BBC GUIDE
TO THE
OLYMPICS

BBC GUIDE
TO THE
OLYMPICS

DAN WADDELL

First published 2000

© Dan Waddell, 2000

The moral right of the author has been asserted.

ISBN 0 563 55171 2

Published by BBC Worldwide Limited,
Woodlands, 80 Wood Lane,
London, W12 0TT

Commissioning Editor: Ben Dunn
Project Editor: Charlotte Heathcote
Designer: Ben Cracknell Studios

Printed and bound by Martins of Berwick Ltd
Cover printed by Belmont Press

The publishers would like to point out that while every effort has been
made to ensure the accuracy and integrity of the text, some information
may have changed by the time of publication.

CONTENTS

INTRODUCTION

It could have been Manchester, instead it's Sydney. In 1993, the Olympic committee decided the sun and sand of Australia's main city were more appealing then the rain and tea of England's northern capital. The decision sent Australians into paroxysms of delight, with Sydney Harbour the scene of wild celebrations. That enthusiasm has not dimmed seven years on. This Olympics has been organized extremely efficiently and promises to be the most spectacular yet. No expense has been spared and, with the Australians' deep love of sport, expectation is running at fever pitch.

The Olympic torch left Greece on 10 May before starting its longest journey ever. By late May it was in Guam, then made its way through Samoa, Papua New Guinea and Fiji followed by a three-day stop-off in New Zealand before hopping across to Australia. Around 12,000 volunteers have been carrying it across Australia, through 1000 towns, over 100 days. Places like Lower Woop Woop and Cootamundra have all been sprucing themselves up for their 15 minutes of fame as the torch passes through their communities. Prior to the Games' start, a few famous names will get involved in an attempt to catch a piece of the Olympic spirit. Golfer Greg Norman will carry the torch across the Sydney Harbour Bridge, while Hollywood star Nicole Kidman will carry it up the stairs to the Opera House.

The Olympics themselves promise a great deal and will be the biggest in history. Two new sports have been added: the triathlon, a lung-bursting event that, because it will be held on the opening day, will provide the Games' first gold medal, and taekwondo, an ancient martial art which dates back about 2000 years. Trampolining has also been added to the gymnastics schedule. Many of the events have been expanded to include women's competitions, among them water polo, weightlifting and the modern pentathlon. Rumours are circulating that women may even have their own wrestling and boxing competitions at the 2004 Games in Athens.

All the world's best athletes will be appearing to try and grab the biggest prize of all, Olympic gold. The support for Australian athletes will be fervent, particularly in the swimming pool, where stars Ian Thorpe and Susie O'Neill are national heroes. The Australians revere their sport stars, who fear letting their fans and country down and so excel on big occasions. Last year was a great one for Australia, winning both the cricket and rugby union World Cups, as well as tennis' Davis Cup. Expect them to challenge the traditional supremacy of the USA in the final medal count.

Britain has a number of gold medal opportunities and will hope to improve on the solitary gold they claimed four years ago in Atlanta. Steve Redgrave, one half of the two-man team that won the gold, is rowing, this time in a strong English foursome; Chris Boardman, who has announced he will retire at the end of the year, is in the cycling; Ben Ainslie is in the sailing; Paula Radcliffe runs in the 10,000m; Denise Lewis goes in the heptathlon and Dean Macey is in the decathlon; Richard Faulds competes in the shooting. All of them have a great chance of success and there are many others who will have a chance to get on the podium if they can rise to the occasion.

Other stories could emerge from the Games, especially on the track. Can Marion Jones, the golden girl of American athletics, win five gold medals in the 100m and 200m, long jump, 4 × 100m relay and 4 × 400m relay? Who will win the tussle between Australian 400m hero Cathy Freeman and the languid Marie-Jose Perec of France? Who will be crowned the fastest man on earth: world record holder Maurice Greene of the USA or reigning Olympic champion Donovan Bailey of Canada? These are just the questions relating to the top established athletes. Each Olympics provides a new hero, someone who has battled to rise from obscurity to the top of their sport. Who will it be in Sydney?

This guide is an attempt to provide fans with the knowledge they need to enjoy every event in the Olympics. For each sport the main rules and regulations are provided, together with the nuances and subtleties that viewers should look out for in the more obscure sports. There are also guides to who is most likely to win the medals in each event, including an event-by-event guide to every race on the track and in the pool.

For the sports that come laden with heaps of impenetrable jargon, a 'Jargon Buster' is provided to help give a clear idea of what the pundits are talking about. The 'Did You Know?' sections for each sport provide titbits on the more bizarre aspects of different events as well as a few strange-but-true stories of past Olympics.

For those who love their statistics, readers will find an all-time top five gold medal table for each sport featured in Sydney and an overall top 10 gold medal table, along with the number of medals that Britain has won in each event.

However, the main aim of the guide is to aid everyone's enjoyment of the first big sports event of the new millennium.

ACKNOWLEDGEMENTS

I would like to thank Ben Dunn and Charlotte Heathcote at BBC Worldwide for all their valuable help and assistance. Many thanks go to those who provided information and improved this guide immeasurably, including: Kevin Hornsey at the British Taekwondo Control Board; Alison Livesey of the British Cycling Federation; Wendy Coles of the Amateur Swimming Federation of Great Britain; John Anderson at the British Canoe Union; Ian Marshall at the International Table Tennis Federation; Kevin Macadam, Great Britain's Baseball General Manager; Toomas Ojasoo at English Volleyball; William Kings at the Badminton Association of England; Mark Woods at *britball.com*; Bill Adcocks at UK Athletics; Henry Budgett at *www.triathloncentral.com* and Neil Parrott at the Grand National Archery Society. If I have forgotten anyone I apologize profusely, but offer my thanks to all that helped out.

THE

Venues

Here is a brief description of each venue to be used in the Sydney 2000 Olympics and the sports to be played at them. Those venues marked with the Olympic rings [QQP] were specifically built for the Games.

Olympic Stadium QQP
The Olympic Stadium is the largest outdoor venue in Olympic history. The stadium, which will hold the opening and closing ceremonies (15 September and 1 October respectively), the athletic events and the football final, holds 110,000 people. It has already hosted an Australia v New Zealand rugby union match that attracted 107,042 – a world record for the sport. In all, it cost around A$690m (£270m). When the Olympics is over, the two temporary open grandstands will be removed, leaving two permanent grandstands, and the capacity will be reduced to 80,000. While the stadium will host the final of the football, the preliminary rounds will be held at the Sydney Football Stadium (cap: 42,000), Melbourne Cricket Ground (cap: 98,000), Brisbane Cricket Ground (cap: 37,000) and the Hindmarsh Stadium in Adelaide (cap: 20,000).

Sydney International Aquatic Centre

The President of the International Olympic Committee, Juan Antonio Samaranch, once described the pool at the aquatic centre as the best he had seen in his life. The centre will play host to the swimming, diving, synchronized swimming, the water polo finals and the swimming leg of the modern pentathlon. The arena holds 17,500 people, while the pool has 10 lanes and is 50 metres long.

Sydney International Regatta Centre ⛢

There was no natural stretch of water suitable for the rowing and canoe/kayak events, so one was built in a former sand and gravel quarry. Around 25,000 native underwater plants have been added, with 12,000 bass fish, 18,000 native trees and 12,000 shrubs. It is one of the Olympics' most scenic venues, with a capacity of 27,000.

Sydney SuperDome ⛢

The SuperDome, the first structure of its type to be built in Australia, has been built in the Sydney Olympic Park. The fully-roofed venue will be the home of the basketball and gymnastics events. The capacity for the former is 18,000 and 15,000 for the latter. Spectators are guaranteed not to miss a moment of the action as four video screens and scoreboards replay much of what takes place. In line with the organizers' guarantee of an ecologically-friendly Games, the whole building is powered by solar energy.

Sydney International Shooting Centre ⛢

The organizers claim that the shooting centre will set the standard for all others to follow. It has three shotgun ranges and holds 7000 spectators.

State Sports Centre

Built in 1984 on the site of an old abattoir, this venue will be the home of the table tennis and taekwondo events, with room for 5000 spectators.

Part of the complex is the State Hockey Centre (cap: 15,000), which is reckoned to be one of the finest hockey venues in the world. The pitch will be resurfaced for the 2000 Games.

The Dome and Pavilions

Usually the Dome and the Pavilions, situated in the Olympic Park, play host to exhibitions, including an annual event every Easter that feature sculptures made from fresh fruit and vegetables.

However, for the Olympics, it will feature more dynamic events, including badminton, basketball, handball, the shooting and fencing events in the modern pentathlon, rhythmic gymnastics and some volleyball matches. The whole venue is equivalent in size to three football pitches, though the Dome will be split into four separate venues for the Games, each holding 10,000 people. The pavilions have a capacity of 6000 each.

Tennis Centre ♋♋♋

The designers of the new No. 1 court at Wimbledon are behind the design of the tennis venue. It features a 10,000-seat centre court, two show courts that can hold 4000 and 2000 people respectively and seven match courts that can take up to 200 people.

All the court surfaces are made of a substance called Rebound Ace cushioned acrylic – the same surface upon which the Australian Open is held.

Sydney Harbour

The picturesque harbour provides the venue for the sailing regatta, allowing an unlimited amount of spectators to see the races – and it's free.

Sydney International Equestrian Centre ⚭⚭

The centre, about 30 miles out of Sydney, is spread over 90 hectares of native bushland, meaning it can hold up to 50,000 spectators.

The showjumping and dressage arenas have been combined, while a 13-kilometre course has been designed for the three-day event. Around 340 stables have been built to house the horses entering the competition, with 260 rooms provided for their grooms.

Sydney Entertainment Centre

Usually this is the venue where all the world's biggest music acts play when they visit Sydney, as it holds 11,000 people. Rather than rock 'n' roll, however, the main show will be the volleyball finals.

Dunc Gray Velodrome ⚭⚭

This newly-constructed venue is named after the first Australian man to win a cycling gold medal, back in 1932. The 250-metre curved track inside the velodrome is made of pine and the building can seat 6000 spectators.

Sydney Convention and Exhibition Centre

Situated in Darling Harbour, the convention centre, with a capacity of 3840, and the five exhibition halls, which hold between 5000 and 10,000 people, is the venue for the wrestling, judo, boxing, weightlifting and fencing events.

Beach Volleyball Centre
A temporary arena has been built on Bondi Beach, which is renowned for its surf, sun and sand – the perfect home for beach volleyball. The arena allows 10,000 people to spectate around a single court. It is the first time the event will be held next to the sea. In Atlanta four years ago, the competition was held miles inland on a specially-created sand court.

Olympic Park Baseball Stadium ♋♋
When it opened in 1998, this 20,000-seater stadium was the first baseball venue of any note that Australia had ever possessed, indicating its growing interest in the sport. When not being used for baseball, its main role is as a showground for cattle during the Royal Easter Show.

Blacktown Olympic Centre at Aquiline Reserve ♋♋
This venue was purpose-built for the softball competition and as a second venue for the baseball tournament. 8000 can see the softball, while 4000 can watch baseball.

Ryde Aquatic Leisure Centre
Short of a venue to host the preliminary rounds of the water polo competition, the organizers turned to a local public swimming pool in a Sydney suburb. Needless to say it is getting a facelift in preparation for the tournament.

Fairfield City Farm
This working farm on the outskirts of Sydney is the home of the seven-kilometre mountain bike course. Around 20,000 people will be able to line the most challenging sections of the course which features steep drops, sharp turns and paths as narrow as 50 centimetres.

MEDAL TABLES

Gold

For each event the top five gold medal winners are listed in order of who has won most. Where there are less than five, it is because there have not been enough gold medals won to list five nations.

Country	Gold Medals
Archery	
1= USA	8
South Korea	8
3= Soviet Union*	1
France	1
Finland	1
Spain	1
Athletics	
1. USA	269
2. Soviet Union*	63
3. West Germany*	38
4= Great Britain	37
Finland	37

Country	Gold Medals
Badminton	
1. South Korea	4
2. Indonesia	3
3= Denmark	1
China	1
Baseball	
1. Cuba	2
Basketball	
1. USA	14
2. Soviet Union*	4
3= Unified Team of former Soviet Union*	1
Yugoslavia	1

* Means country no longer appears in the Olympics under that name. The medal count for Germany includes medals won prior to World War Two and after reunification.

Country	Gold Medals	Country	Gold Medals

Boxing
1. USA — 47
2. Cuba — 23
3= Italy — 14
   Soviet Union* — 14
5. Great Britain — 12

Canoe/Kayak
1. Soviet Union* — 28
2. West Germany* — 15
3. Germany — 11
4. Sweden — 10
5. Hungary — 9

Cycling
1. Italy — 23
2. France — 20
3. Soviet Union* — 7
4. Netherlands — 6
5= West Germany* — 5
   Germany — 5
   Australia — 5

Diving
1. USA — 46
2. China — 9
3. West Germany* — 5
4= Sweden — 4
   Soviet Union* — 4

Equestrian
1. Sweden — 17
2. East Germany* — 16
3. Germany — 15
4. France — 10
5. USA — 8

Fencing
1. Italy — 36
2= France — 32
   Hungary — 32
4. Soviet Union* — 18
5. East Germany* — 8

Football
1= Great Britain — 3
   Hungary — 3
3= Soviet Union* — 2
   Uruguay — 2
5= USA — 1
   West Germany* — 1
   Italy — 1
   Nigeria — 1
   France — 1
   Sweden — 1
   Czechoslovakia* — 1
   Poland — 1
   Canada — 1
   Spain — 1
   Belgium — 1
   Yugoslavia — 1

Gymnastics
1. Soviet Union* — 73
2. Japan — 27
3. USA — 17
4. Romania — 16
5. Switzerland — 15

Handball
1. Soviet Union* — 4
2. Yugoslavia — 3
3. South Korea — 2

Country	Gold Medals
4= Unified Team	
of former Soviet Union*	1
Denmark	1
Croatia	1
West Germany*	1

Hockey
1. India	8
2= Pakistan	3
Great Britain	3
4= Netherlands	2
Australia	2

Judo
1. Japan	17
2. France	8
3. South Korea	7
4. Soviet Union*	5
5= Poland	3
Cuba	3

Modern Pentathlon
1. Sweden	9
2. Hungary	4
3. Poland	2
4= Soviet Union*	1
Italy	1
Germany	1
Kazakhstan	1

Rowing
1= USA	25
West Germany*	25
3. Great Britain	17
4. Soviet Union	11
5= Germany	10
Romania	10

Country	Gold Medals

Sailing
1. USA	9
2= Denmark	7
Spain	7
4. France	5
5= Brazil	4
New Zealand	4

Shooting
1. USA	21
2. Soviet Union*	11
3. Italy	8
4. China	6
5= France	5
Hungary	5
Germany	5
East Germany	5
Romania	5
Unified Team	
of former Soviet Union*	5

Softball
1. USA	1

Swimming
1. USA	175
2. Australia	39
3. West Germany*	38
4. Hungary	22
5. Japan	15

Table Tennis
1. China	9
2. South Korea	2
3. Sweden	1

Country	Gold Medals
Tennis	
1. USA	13
2. Great Britain	10
3. South Africa	3
4= France	2
Germany	2
Volleyball	
1. Soviet Union*	7
2= USA	3
Japan	3
4= Cuba	2
Brazil	2
Water Polo	
1. Hungary	6
2. Great Britain	4

Country	Gold Medals
3= Italy	3
Yugoslavia	3
5. Soviet Union*	2
Weightlifting	
1. Soviet Union*	39
2. USA	14
3. Bulgaria	10
4. France	9
5. China	6
Wrestling	
1. Soviet Union*	62
2. USA	46
3. Sweden	27
4. Finland	26
5. Japan	20

TOP TEN ALL TIME

GOLD MEDAL TABLES

This table is calculated by counting only those gold medals won in sports featured in the Sydney Games.

1. USA	723	6. France	117
2. Soviet Union*	377	7. Great Britain	115
3. West Germany*	148	8. Germany	101
4. Italy	136	9. Sweden	96
5. Hungary	132	10. Japan	91

THE
Events

Archery

17 – 22 September, International Archery Park

For most people, archery conjures up images of medieval battles, when the bow and arrow was the most important weapon in an army's arsenal. This image is partly true – few sports are as old as this one. Historians have estimated that archery was first used 25,000 years ago for hunting and warfare. Later, in the Middle Ages (AD500 – AD1500), particularly in England, the bow and arrow became indispensible. That history is still honoured in the modern sport: when an arrow already stuck in the target has its shaft split by another incoming arrow it is known as a 'Robin Hood', in honour of the famous English outlaw who mythically won a contest by firing his arrow into his opponent's one. However, little about archery today resembles that practised by Robin Hood's Merry Men. Fibreglass bows have replaced wooden ones and the arrows – usually made of carbon graphite or aluminium – can travel at up to 150mph as they hurtle towards the target. But two basic skills have remained unchanged; developing a good eye and a steady arm.

Despite its ancient, illustrious history, archery disappeared off the Olympic schedule in 1920, simply because the rules of the sport were so inconsistent and contests at each of the pre-1920 Games varied widely. Indeed, at the 1900 Games in Paris, the target for the archers was live pigeons. The sport went into abeyance for more than 50 years before being reinstated for the 1972 Munich Games with a uniform set of rules still recognizable today. The sport has since been dominated by the USA, and in Justin Huish, who won gold in Atlanta in 1996 aged only 21, the sport has a young star who, with his pony-tail, baseball cap and shades, has an outlaw image that Robin Hood himself would be proud of.

WHAT TO **WATCH**

Men's bows are usually 1.83 metres long, while women's bows cannot be longer than 1.6 metres. The arrow itself, which has a maximum diameter of 11 millimetres, is between 61 and 81 centimetres long and is held on the string of the bow before firing, by a device called a nock. The feathers on the back of the arrow – though often made of plastic – are there to stabilize its flight and are called fletching. The archer must take a stance 70 metres from the target and nock the arrow to the string. The arm must be very steady and very strong to draw the arrow back under the chin, which is usually done using three fingers. Then the archer looks through the sight mounted on the bow and lines up the target. For the arrow to fly straight, all fingers must release the arrow simultaneously. Strength is an important aspect of the sport; It takes 50 pounds of pressure to pull the arrow back to the firing position and any waver can cause the arrow to go off line in a sport where the slightest wobble can be the difference between success and failure. Then, quickly, the process must be repeated.

WHAT ARE THE **RULES?**

The competition format has been redesigned in recent years so that competitors advance through the rounds by eliminating the opposition in sudden-death, head-to-head battles. There are two types of competition – team and individual play. Firstly, the competitors are given an order of play drawn by a computer for the purpose of ranking them and to determine seedings. This is called a ranking round. 64 men and 64 women compete separately, shooting 12 'ends' of six arrows each within a time limit of four minutes per end. The scores they achieve determine their seeding, between 1 and 64. This applies for both the individual and team events, the format for which are as follows:

Individual events: Elimination begins with the no. 1 seed playing no. 64, no. 2 plays no. 63 and so on. Each of the archers shoots six ends of three arrows within a time limit of forty seconds per arrow. If an archer fails to fire an arrow within that time then their highest scoring arrow of that end is not counted, as a penalty. This format continues until only four competitors remain to take part in the semi-finals, when only four ends of three arrows are played to determine who picks up the medals.

Team events: The ranking round scores are vital. The top 16 nations, based on each country's total score in the ranking round, go forward into the elimination round. Three archers in each team shoot an end of nine arrows within a time limit of three minutes (only 20 seconds per arrow) – half the time allowed in the individual event. The top four teams contest the medals.

All archers must fire from a standing position, providing they are physically able to. In 1984, New Zealander Neroli

Fairhall competed from a wheelchair, finishing 35th, as did the Italian Paola Fantato at Atlanta four years ago. The arrows must be marked with the competitor's name or initials to distinguish them from others when scoring takes place. If an archer misfires and the arrow falls to the ground within reach it can be fired again. If it is out of reach, the misfire counts as a shot and cannot be taken again. In the team events, archers can receive coaching while at the shooting line, but that luxury is forbidden during the individual events.

The target has 10 scoring zones, defined by 10 rings. The highest score is 10 points for hitting the centre ring, which is 12.2 centimetres wide and, as in darts, is known as the bullseye. Within the bullseye is an inner ring called the X10, which is still worth only 10 points, but is used to decide ties if scores are equal; the player with the most X10s advances through to the next round. Moving out from the centre, each ring is worth one point less than the previous one, with the lowest score on the target being one point. The two innermost rings are gold in colour, including the X10. In order, going away from the centre two rings at a time, the other colours are red, blue, black and white. Should an arrow become embedded in another already in the board, a 'Robin Hood', then the score of the first arrow is taken, while if an arrow splits the line dividing two rings then the highest point score is taken. The player with most points wins the tie.

WHO WILL **WIN?**

Britain has won two gold medals in archery, but they are unlikely to add to that tally in Sydney. Since 1972, the USA has dominated the men's competition, winning six gold medals. Justin Huish may make it seven. In the women's competition, South Korea have dominated, picking up seven golds since 1972, including both the individual and team gold at the last three Olympics. However, their star, Kim Kyung-wook, is not travelling to Sydney, so expect the Germans to put up a strong fight.

JARGON BUSTER

End: A group of arrows that are scored together.

Finger tab: A piece of leather worn to protect the string fingers when the arrow is released.

Fletching: The feathers attached to the arrow that stabilize it during flight.

Limb: The part of the bow from the handle to the tip.

Nock: The attachment on the rear end of an arrow that holds it in place on the bowstring, or the act of placing the arrow on the string.

Riser: The handle of the bow. The side facing the target is the back. The side near the string is the belly.

Robin Hood: When an archer drives the tip of one arrow deep into the end of another arrow already stuck in the target.

Sight: A mechanical device placed on the bow to help the archer aim.

Stabilizer: A weight mounted on a bow, usually extending some distance from the handle, that helps minimize undesirable movement of the bow string upon release.

DID YOU **KNOW?**

- From where the archers stand the target, which is 1.22 metres in diameter, looks the size of the head of a thumbtack held at arm's length, while the bullseye, which stands 1.3 metres above the ground, looks no larger than a pinhole.

- The only time that an American did not win an individual gold in the men's event was in 1992.

BRITISH MEDAL COUNT

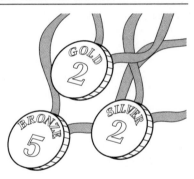

Athletics

The most eagerly-awaited events at the Games will be on the track. The men's 100 metres final generates more excitement than any other, as the sprinters compete to gain the accolade of 'fastest man on earth'. The newly-constructed Olympic Stadium will be crammed all day, every day as the best athletes in the world compete for the ultimate prize – Olympic gold. Michael Johnson, Maurice Greene, Colin Jackson, Marion Jones, Cathy Freeman, Hicham El Guerrouj, Haile Gebreselassie, Jonathan Edwards and Gail Devers are just a few of the world-class athletes that will be on show. It is a stunning line-up that is set to give us one of the most exciting track and field Olympics ever. Mini-dramas will be present everywhere: can Colin Jackson and Jonathan Edwards crown their careers with their first Olympic gold medals? Can Cathy Freeman take the 400m gold in front of her adoring home crowd? Will Marion Jones live up to her billing and take the 100m and 200m titles, perhaps even the long jump as well? Can Michael Johnson go even faster? Will Denise Lewis and Dean Macey continue to improve in the heptathlon and decathlon? Only time will tell.

Archery - Justin Huish (USA)

Athletics - Colin Jackson (GBR), **110m Hurdles**

Athletics - Jonathan Edwards (GBR), **Triple Jump**

Athletics - Dean Macey (GBR), **Decathlon**

Athletics - Iwan Thomas
(GBR), **400m**

Athletics - Steve
Backley (GBR),
Javelin

Athletics - Denise Lewis (GBR), **Heptathlon**

Athletics - Paula Radcliffe (GBR), **Long Distance events**

Athletics - Maurice
Greene (USA), **Sprint**

Athletics -
Michael Johnson
(USA), **Sprint**

Athletics - Marion Jones (USA), **Sprint and Long Jump**

Athletics - Cathy Freeman (AUS), **400m**

Athletics - Marie-José Perec (FRA), **400m**

Canoeing - Paul Ratcliffe (GBR)

Athletics is the purest form of sport in the Games. Athletes compete to run fastest, throw furthest, and jump higher, just as they did thousands of years ago at the birth of the Olympics in ancient Greece. The original Olympic champion was Coroebus who, in 776 BC, won the sprint down the length of the stadium, a distance of 193 metres. Running races were always the highlight of the ancient Games, though often the competitors were made to dress up in suits of armour or carry weapons. Racing resurfaced in the nineteenth century, when the universities of Oxford and Cambridge held the first modern track meeting in 1864. The sport took off in England and in 1896 was included in the first modern Games, on a course designed by an Englishman. The races included the 100m, 400m, 800m, 1500m and the marathon, which are all still part of athletics more than a century later. No event has a greater or more controversial history than the marathon. According to legend, the race is based upon the efforts of a Greek soldier who ran 25 miles to carry news of the Battle of Marathon. After delivering the news, he dropped dead. In 1908, in London, the race was extended to 26 miles and 385 yards so it could finish in view of the British royal family. Indeed, royalty got a King's eye view of one of the Games' most famous controversies. Derando Pietri of Italy entered the stadium in the lead but collapsed numerous times around the track, and was helped up. Eventually race officials carried him over the line just as American Johnny Hayes entered the stadium. Amid ugly scenes of fights breaking out in the stands and American officials rowing furiously with the British judges, Pietri was disqualified.

Women's athletics events were introduced in 1928, but were curtailed when a number of competitors collapsed after the 800m race. As a result, women were banned from running distances over 200m for the next 32 years. However, good sense was restored in 1960, and men and women now compete over similar distances. In 1996, women got their own triple jump competition, and in Sydney there are, for the first time, women's competitions in the pole vault and hammer throw.

Jumping and throwing have also been part of the ancient Olympic tradition. Discus and spear throwing were part of the ancient Games, though the spear is now a javelin and the aim is distance, not accuracy. The long jump was also an event in the ancient Games, as it was in 1896 alongside the high jump, triple jump and the pole vault. The high jump is the only discipline to have changed considerably over the years, with the introduction of the 'Fosbury Flop', a technique that replaced the old scissors jump. It was named after its originator, Dick Fosbury, who won gold in 1968 by flying backwards over the bar. The same Games saw the establishment of one of the longest-standing world records in history. Bob Beamon's incredible leap of 8.90 metres in the long jump shattered the former record by 65 centimetres. Amazingly, this record stood until 1991, when the American, Mike Powell, finally broke it.

Another event with a great history is the decathlon (the 10-event competition), which many people view as the contest to become the world's greatest all-round athlete. In ancient Greece, it was a pentathlon (five-event competition), held as an elimination contest, with only the top two competitors going into the final event – a wrestling match to decide the winner. Now, it is a gruelling two-day test featuring 10 events, though Britain's legendary decathlete Daley Thompson once jokingly dubbed it as 'nine Mickey Mouse events and a 1500m run'. Dean Macey could be the new Daley Thompson.

The women's pentathlon started in 1964 but in 1984 became the heptathlon (seven-event competition), making it more demanding.

Sadly, drug-taking has marred previous athletics competitions. The IAAF, the athletics world governing body, has been attempting to crack down on dope cheats and the signs are that in major competitions its strategy is paying off. However, there is still a lot of suspicion surrounding the sport, and it needs a good, clean Olympics to retain its credibility.

WHAT TO **WATCH**

Athletics can be divided into four categories: track, road, field and combined events. The track events comprise the sprints over 100m, 200m, and 400m; middle distance events, the 800m and 1500m; and long distance events, the 5000m and 10,000m. The hurdle events are the 110m and 400m for men and 100m and 400m for women. All relays involve teams of four runners. There is also the men's 3000m steeplechase. Relay races take place over 100m and 400m.

The field events are made up of the long jump, triple jump, high jump, pole vault, javelin, discus, shot-put and the hammer. The road events are the marathon, the men's 20km and 50km walk, and the women's 10km walk, while the combined events are made up of the heptathlon for women and decathlon for men.

Here is a rough guide to what to look out for in the main events:

Sprints and Relays
Runners drive out of the blocks, and aim to get into their stride quickly. They try to attain top speed as soon as possible

and then maintain it, lifting their knees and pumping their legs. Expect the winner in the men's races to come home in the 100m in under 10 seconds, probably the time it has taken you to read this paragraph up to this point. In the 200m and 400m events, the runners have a staggered bend to contend with. The inside lane (lane one) is the tightest to run around, and is the least favoured draw, particularly for the bigger men, although the outside lane (lane eight) is similarly disliked since it is impossible to see your fellow competitors until they are overtaking you. Runners have to get through a series of heats and semi-finals to reach the final and are careful not to expend too much energy along the way. In the relays, a baton is passed between team-mates. It is vital that this passing is done smoothly to avoid losing precious tenths of seconds.

Middle and Long Distance Events

Where the sprints are explosive and dynamic, the 800m, 1500m, 5000m and 10,000m are much more tactical. Strategy plays an integral part. Where should a runner position him or herself in the pack to avoid being boxed in by other competitors? When should the final dash for the line be started? Break away too soon and he or she will tire and be caught by the others, but go too late and the race will be over. Those with a good sprint finish will bide their time and simply keep in contention with the leaders until the final lap, or even the final bend, while the slower finishers will push the pace during the race to sap the energy of their quick-sprinting opponents.

Hurdles

Stride pattern is everything in the 110m, 100m and 400m hurdles. The runner's front leg should pass over the barrier with the trailing leg coming through to propel him or her on to the next obstacle. If the stride pattern becomes irregular then rhythm and speed are lost. Clipping the top of a hurdle is not too great a problem, but hitting one hard can throw the runner off balance and force them to lose their stride pattern. In the 110m for men and 100m for women, hurdlers go flat out from the start, and have to be wary in their heats not to relax too much and trip over a hurdle. The 400m event has more scope for runners to compose themselves, and gradually build up rhythm and speed for the finish.

Jumping

There are two horizontal jumps, the long and triple jump, and two vertical ones, the high jump and pole vault. The secret of long jump success is in the speed of the run-up. Jumpers aim to hit a board placed in the runway before the sand pit at top speed, without overstepping it (since this is a foul jump), then use their arms and legs to propel themselves through the air for as long as possible before landing with their legs out in front of them. Speed also plays a part in the triple jump, allowing the competitors to hop, step and jump at full tilt. Again, they pull back with the arms as they move through the air to squeeze every inch out of the jump.

In the high jump, the take-off point is vital. Too close and the jumper will clip the bar on the way up, too far away and the jumper will hit the bar on the way down. High jumpers use the front leg to leap in the air and then arch their backs over the bar before pulling their legs up, the Fosbury Flop. The slightest contact with the bar can make it wobble. On a good day it stays in place, on a bad day it falls. The pole vault requires the athlete to plant his pole in a box under the bar to generate tremendous leverage and propel him into the air. The pole bends dramatically then straightens up to carry the jumper over the bar. The athletes approach the bar feet first, upside down and at the point when the pole is fully extended they push themselves off and arch over the bar. Timing is crucial.

Throwing

The athlete who throws farthest wins, but to achieve this, technique and timing are vital. If an athlete gets everything right then the object thrown will soar through the air. Get it wrong and quite often he or she will step over the foul line on purpose to invalidate the throw. In the javelin, the athlete needs to get his throwing arm working perfectly to allow the javelin to fly at the right trajectory, with little or no flutter (vibration) as it is in flight. Some throwers have short run-ups and all their power comes from having a fast arm, though the pressure on the shoulder and elbow can be massive and injury is always a threat. In the shot put, discus and hammer, the preserve of the heavyweight athletes, the ability to glide quickly and smoothly across the throwing circle is essential in order to generate the maximum amount of lift and distance.

WHAT ARE THE **RULES?**

Here is a list of the major rules that apply in certain events:

- Runners must stay within their lanes for all sprints (the 110m, 100m, and 400m hurdles and the 4 × 100m relay). In the 4 × 400m relay, athletes can break out of their lanes after reaching the 'breakline' on the second leg.

- Two false starts result in disqualification. For distances of up to 400m, athletes must use a crouch start from blocks. For the longer distances, they use a standing start.

- In all relays, the runners must exchange batons within a 20-metre takeover zone. Even after handing over the baton, runners must stay within their lanes until the race is over or face disqualification. If the baton is dropped only the person who dropped it can pick it up again.

- A sprint, hurdle or triple and long jump world record will not count if the wind speed is greater than two metres per second behind the athlete.

- In the walking races, a walker must have at least one foot on the ground at all times. Nine judges around the course watch the walkers and can caution one if they feel they are breaking the rules. If three judges warn a walker then he or she is disqualified.

- If two competitors tie in the high jump or pole vault, there are two methods to decide the winner. First, which athlete needed the fewest jumps to clear the winning height, and if that is the same, which athlete failed fewest jumps overall. If that is still the same, then the athletes are awarded the same placing, unless they are competing for the gold medal, in which case there is a jump-off. Athletes jump at the height at which they finally failed. If they both clear this height, the bar is raised, while if they fail the bar is lowered until a victor emerges.

- Any tie in the long jump or triple jump means the second best jumps of the athletes are compared and the best one wins. If it is still not resolved, then the third best jumps are compared, and so on. If a tie still remains after all jumps have been compared then the tie stands, unless a gold medal is at stake, in which case the athletes carry on competing until the tie is broken.

- High jumpers and pole vaulters can choose to pass or jump at a height. They are eliminated if they fail to clear the bar three times in succession.

- Judges can penalize an athlete for exceeding the specified time limit for a jump and that attempt is disallowed. However, if the athlete sets off for the jump before their time is up, the jump is still valid.

WHO WILL **WIN?**

Predicting who will win athletics events a few months in advance is always a difficult exercise considering how many athletes are prone to injury and may not end up taking part. However, it is worth going through each event and mentioning the names of those, who if they do make it to Sydney in good condition, will be among the favourites for the medals. Britain has a number of good medal candidates who had to attain the Olympic qualifying criteria laid down by the British Athletics Association. Here, then, is a prediction for each event.

100m, men   Maurice Greene (USA)
                           1999, 9.79secs

Donovan Bailey of Canada is attempting to work his way back from injury in order to be fit enough to defend the gold medal he won so impressively in Atlanta. He will have to be at his peak to see off what will be a hugely talented field. The favourite must be world record holder and world champion Maurice Greene, who looked unstoppable last year. Trinidadian Atol Boldon and Bruny Surin of Canada are medal hopes, together with British pair Jason Gardener and Dwain

Chambers. In 1999, the latter became only the second European sprinter, after Linford Christie, to go under 10 seconds and then grabbed a bronze at the World Championships in Seville. Gardener finished a disappointing seventh in that race, but was recovering from food poisoning at the time. The best is yet to come from both of them, and their rivalry should spur each other on, though a bronze could be about the best they can expect in such a high-quality field.

100m, women   Florence Griffith-Joyner (USA)
1988, 10.49secs

This could be the Games when American Marion Jones emulates the great American Carl Lewis and goes for gold in the 100m, 200m, the 4 × 100m relay and the long jump. Her whole season's training and performing is geared towards being at her peak for Sydney. If she is at her best then she should win the 100m, though compatriot Inge Miller will be a close challenger. Gail Devers, a veteran of the last two Olympics, will be in the hunt for a medal, as will Ekaterini Thanou of Greece.

200m, men   Michael Johnson (USA)
1996, 19.32secs

No one knows whether Johnson will attempt to win both the 200m and 400m gold medals to crown his remarkable career. He may choose to settle for the 400m only, in which case the 200m runners will breathe a sigh of relief. Many of the faces from the 100m will appear once again; Boldon and Greene will compete, along with the experienced Frankie Fredericks of Namibia and Francis Obikwelu of Nigeria. Julian Golding and Marlon Devonish of Britain will be looking to reach the final, though a medal might be beyond them.

200m, women   Florence Griffith-Joyner (USA)
1988, 21.34secs

The winner should almost certainly be either Marion Jones or Inge Miller, both of the USA. In 1999, the pair clocked the 11 fastest times at this distance between them. No one else should come close, though Andrea Phillip of Germany carries Europe's best hope of a medal.

400m, men   Michael Johnson (USA)
1999, 43.18secs

World champion and world record holder Johnson looks unstoppable at this event, and unless there is a major shock the rest are running for silver and bronze. One of those could be Britain's Iwan Thomas, European and Commonwealth champion. He has not looked back since finishing fifth in Atlanta four years ago, aged 22. Last year was massively frustrating for him, as ankle surgery ruled him out for almost the whole season. If he has prepared well, and found some form in the early part of the 2000 season there is no reason why he should not collect a medal. Mark Richardson is another Briton who will be looking to get a place, but both he and Thomas will have to beat off strong challenges from Jerome Young of the USA and Sanderlei Parrela of Brazil.

400m, women   Marita Koch (former GDR)
1985, 47.60secs

This event could provide one of the most dramatic tussles in any event of the whole Games. World champion Cathy Freeman, Australia's greatest ever sprinter and a national hero, could face the French defending gold medallist Marie-Jose Perec, who has struggled with injury recently. The noise inside the stadium will be deafening.

However, if those two concentrate too much on each other, Anja Rucker of Germany could be in the frame and, with improvement, so could Britain's Katherine Merry. She started her career over 100m and 200m but last year moved up to 400m and impressed everyone by reaching the finals of the World Championships where she finished fifth. It was only her first year competing in the event, and there should be more success to come.

| **800m, men** | Wilson Kipketer (DEN) |
| | 1997, 1 min 41.11secs |

World champion and record holder Kipketer is favourite to win this event, though he will be pushed hard by South Africa's Hezekiel Sepeng. The best European hope lies with Switzerland's Andre Bucher, while the Kenyans always provide an impressive newcomer. Likely British contenders are Curtis Robb and John Mayock, neither of whom has shown anything like their true potential at the highest level. A place in the final would be a good start.

| **800m, women** | Jarmila Kratochvilova (CZE) |
| | 1983, 1min 53.28secs |

This may be a three-way battle between Marie Mutola of Mozambique, world champion Ludmila Formanova of the Czech Republic and Svetlana Matserkova of Russia. The three fought hard in last year's World Championships with the Czech coming out on top.

1500m, men   Hicham El Guerrouj (MAR)
1998, 3mins 26.00secs

Moroccan El Guerrouj, who also holds the world record for the mile, looks unbeatable in this event on current form. The Kenyans will provide him with the stiffest challenge, probably in the form of either Noah Ngeny or Barnard Lagat. The best European hope lies with the Spaniards Reyes Estevez and Fermin Cacho.

1500m, women   Qu Yunxia (CHN)
1993, 3mins 50.46secs

This should be a very open race. Masterkova of Russia is the world champion, and American Regina Jacobs could be in line for a medal, but there is also a chance for Britain's Kelly Holmes to shine if she is back to her best. She had a difficult time with injuries in 1999, but now looks to be finding her form. She may well decide to 'double up' and race in the 800m as well.

5000m, men   Haile Gebreselassie (ETH)
1998, 12mins 39.36secs

The king of long-distance running, Gebreselassie has to be the favourite for this event. The little man from Ethiopia can run any distance he wants, and may attempt to race in both the 5000m and 10,000m, though this may over-stretch him. Whichever one he picks, don't bet against him. His rivals will almost all be Kenyans such as Daniel Komen and Paul Tergat, though the main beneficiary, should the Ethiopian concentrate on the 10,000m only, will be world champion Salah Missou of Morocco.

5000m, women   Jiang Bo (CHN)
                            1997, 14mins 28.09secs

World champion Gabriala Szabo is highly fancied in this event. The Romanian's main threat will come from Zalra Ouaziz of Morocco and Irina Mikitenko of Germany.

10,000m, men   Haile Gebreselassie (ETH)
                            1998, 26mins 22.75secs

If he runs it, Gebreselassie should win it. The Kenyans, Paul Tergat and Paul Koech are his closest rivals. Europe's best medal hope is probably Antonio Pinto of Portugal, though a lot depends on the weather. If it's hot, then the Africans should reign supreme.

10,000m, women   Wang Junxia (CHN)
                            1993, 29mins 21.78secs

Paula Radcliffe of Great Britain has a superb chance of a medal. She is by far the best long-distance women's runner the UK has produced since Liz McColgan, though she will be praying the weather is cool. She ran brilliantly to take the 1999 World Championship silver medal, pushing the winner, Geta Wami of Ethiopia, all the way to the line. Wami is her main rival once again, along with Tegla Laroupe of Kenya.

110m hurdles, men   Colin Jackson (GBR)
                            1993, 12.91secs

Jackson, one of the greatest athletes in the history of British athletics, bounced back to his best form in 1999, winning the World Championship title in Seville. The Olympic crown is the only one that eludes him and he will be desperate to win it in what will almost certainly be his last Olympics. His main threat will come from a trio of Americans, Mark Crear, Larry Wade and Allen Johnson, and Cuban Anier Garcia.

100m hurdles, women   Yordanka Donkova (BUL)
1988, 12.21secs

Gail Devers, the veteran American, will be seeking to defend her 1999 World Championship title, which showed she can still compete with the best. Her rivals include Nigeria's Glory Alozie, Kazakhstan's Olga Shishigina and another veteran, Ludmila Enqvist of Sweden.

400m hurdles, men   Kevin Young (USA)
1992, 46.78secs

It seems that the American domination of this event has ended, ushering in the European challengers. World champion Fabrizio Mori of Italy, Stephane Diagana of France and Marcel Schelbert of Switzerland are among the contenders in a very open race. Britain's Chris Rawlinson will be looking to make the final.

400m hurdles, women   Kim Batten (USA)
1995, 52.61secs

Like the men's event, this could be another very open race. Daimi Perma of Cuba, Nezha Bidouane of Morocco and Jamaica's Deon Hemmings should all contest the medals, together with Ionela Tirlea of Romania, who will lead the European charge.

3000m steeplechase, men Bernard Barmasai (KEN)
1997, 7 mins 55.72secs

World record holder Barmasai is the favourite for this one, though he faces strong challenges from his fellow Kenyans, notably Christopher Koskei and Paul Kosgei.

Marathon, men World's best performance*:
Khalid Khannouchi (MAR)
1999, 2hrs 5mins 42secs

(*There are no World Records because marathons are run on a variety of courses.)

The marathon is an almost impossible event in which to predict a winner. Look out for the Kenyans, Moses Tanui and Juphet Kosgei, South Africa's Gert Thyss – the winner of the Tokyo marathon – and the winner of the 1999 London marathon, Moroccan Abdelkader El Mouaziz. Britain's representative is likely to be Jon Brown, who finished fourth in the 1999 London event.

Marathon, women World's best performance:
Tegla Laroupe (KEN)
1999, 2hrs 20mins 43secs

Like the men's race, this is a difficult event to forecast. Although Laroupe may not choose to enter this event, the winner is almost certain to come from Africa. Joyce Chopchunka of Kenya, the winner of the women's race in the 1999 London marathon, is a possible victor, as is Fatuma Roba of Ethiopia. For an outside bet, watch Australian Nicole Carroll, who will be boosted by her home crowd, will be familiar with the weather conditions, and will know Sydney's streets.

High jump, men

Javier Sotomayor (CUB)
1993, 2m 45cm

The world record holder, Sotomayor, is likely to take part in Sydney but his air of invincibility has gone and he looks past his best. This leaves the door open for Britain's Steve Smith, who won bronze four years ago, and has the ability to do better. The man from Liverpool is a superb competitor and a match for anyone in the world. If he is in form, he is one of our best medal chances. His main threat comes from world champion Vyacheslav Voronin of Russia and Martin Buss of Germany.

High jump, women

Stefka Kostadinova (BUL)
1987, 2m 9cm

This is a very open competition with the eastern European trio of Inga Babakova and Yelena Yelesina, from Russia, and Svetlana Lapina of the Ukraine among the medal contenders. Another good bet is South African Hestrie Strobeck-Clorte – another athlete from a nation slowly making its mark on the athletics world.

Pole vault, men

Segey Bubka (RUS)
1994, 6m 14cm

It would be very surprising if Maksim Tarasov, Bubka's heir, did not win gold in this event. Should he slip up, then Jeff Hartwig of the USA and Dmitry Markov of Australia will be waiting to cash in.

Pole vault, women   Emma George (AUS) and
Stacy Dragila (USA), 1999, 4m 60cm

The two world record holders will be competing, with George looking to do well in front of her home crowd. Dragila will be hoping to add the first women's Olympic pole vault crown to last year's world title, where she equalled George's world record. Another contender is Anzhela Balakhonova of the Ukraine.

Long jump, men   Mike Powell (USA)
1991, 8m 95cm

The red-hot favourite is spring-heeled Cuban Ivan Pedroso, the world champion. His only real threats come from Jamaica's James Beckford and Yago Lamela of Spain.

Long jump, women   Galina Chistyakova (RUS)
1988, 7m 52cm

Former Briton, Fiona May, now representing Italy, is in the hunt for gold, though she will have to overcome Spain's world champion, Niurka Montalvo. The interest in this event lies with Marion Jones. If she wins gold then she is on her way to equalling Carl Lewis's achievement of four gold medals in a single Olympics.

Triple jump, men   Jonathan Edwards (GBR)
1995, 18m 29cm

Edwards at his best is unbeatable. He was pipped by the American Kenny Harrison four years ago, to his great disappointment, and last year was only third in the World

Championships behind Charles Friedek and Rostislav Dimitrov of Bulgaria. He needs to recapture the wondrous form of 1995 when he never looked like being beaten and won BBC's Sports Personality of the Year.

Triple jump, women　　　　Inessa Kravets (UKR)
1995, 15m 50cm

British fans will be hoping that Ashia Hansen fulfils her obvious potential and gets among the medals, though it will be difficult. The hot favourite is Greece's Paraskevi Tsiamata, the world champion, who was almost unbeaten during 1999. Other rivals include Yamile Aldama of Cuba and Yelena Govorova of the Ukraine.

Shot put, men　　　　Randy Barnes (USA)
1990, 23m 12cm

The Americans John Godina and world champion C.J. Hunter should both do well, together with Oliver Sven-Buder of Germany.

Shot put, women　　　　Natalya Lisovskaya (RUS)
1987, 22m 63cm

Look out for Svetlana Krivelyova of Russia and the German pair Astrid Kimbermuss and Nadine Kleinert.

Discus, men　　　　Jurgen Schult (GER)
1986, 74m 8cm

Jurgen Schult is still around, 14 years after posting his world record throw. In last year's World Championships he finished second behind Anthony Washington of the USA, his main

rival in Sydney. Another veteran hoping to win gold is
Germany's Lars Riedel.

Discus, women   Gabriele Reinsch (GER)
                                    1988, 76m 8cm*

(*Women achieve greater distances than men because their discus is a kilogram lighter.)

In an open event, the winner may come from one of the
following: Franka Dietzsch, the German world champion,
Nicoleta Grasu of Romania, Natalya Sadova of Russia and
Anastasia Kelesidou of Greece.

Hammer, men   Yurly Sedykh (RUS)
                                    1986, 86m 74cm

Tibor Gecsek and Adrian Amus (Hungary), and Karsten Kobs
(Germany), are likely to be among the medallists in this
event.

Hammer, women   Mihaela Milente (ROM)
                                    1998, 73m 14cm

If all goes to plan, the first ever women's Olympic hammer
champion will be Mihaela Milente, holder of the world title
and the world record. Her nearest rival is Olga Kuzenkova of
Russia. Lorraine Shaw could represent Britain.

Javelin, men   Jan Zelezny (CZE)
                                    1996, 98m 48cm

Steve Backley of Great Britain has already confirmed himself
one of the all-time javelin greats, but he would dearly love an
Olympic title to sit beside his European and Commonwealth

crowns. He won silver four years ago and will be hoping to go one better this time. Last year saw him struggling with his technique, though he still managed to throw over 83 metres in every competition he entered. Let's hope the flaws are ironed out in time for Sydney and he avoids injury. He will be up against world champion Ari Parviainen of Finland, world record holder Jan Zelezny of the Czech Republic, Boris Henry of Germany, and fellow Briton, Mick Hill, who has lived in Backley's shadow most of his career but is a superb competitor. It should be a riveting competition.

| **Javelin, women** | Trine Solberg-Hattestad (NOR) |
| | 1999, 68m 19cm |

Hattestad is a favourite here, though she only managed third in last year's World Championships. Tatyana Shilolenko of Russia and Osleidys Henendez of Cuba are also leading contenders.

| **Decathlon** | Tomas Dvorak (CZE) |
| | 1999, 8994 points |

Dvorak is the clear favourite, but all British eyes will be on Dean Macey to see if he can recreate his superb perform-ance to win silver behind the Czech at the World Champion-ships in Seville last year. He only completed his first decathlon at the end of May 1999, which makes his achievement even more remarkable. In Seville, he set six personal bests on his senior international debut making him a national hero overnight. How he copes with the expectation will be interesting, but he has the ability to become the first British gold medallist in the decathlon since Daley Thompson. Chris

Huffins of the USA and Sebastien Levicq of France will be challenging him for a medal spot.

Heptathlon Jackie Joyner-Kersee (USA)
1988, 7291 points

Britain's most talented all-round athlete Denise Lewis is going for gold in the heptathlon. She appears to improve each year, and last summer grabbed the silver at the World Championships. In Atlanta in 1996 she was our only female medallist, and is probably our best chance of gold among the women in Sydney. She will need to improve on her personal best to win the title, but that is not beyond her. She must overcome her conqueror in Seville, Eunice Barber of France, and see off Ghada Shouaa of Syria and Shandra Nathan of the USA, but it is within her capabilities.

4 × 100m relay, men USA
1993, 37.40secs

Great Britain have a good medal chance with a team likely to feature Jason Gardener, Darren Campbell, Marlon Devonish and Dwain Chambers. The USA are favourites to win, though Canada and Nigeria are also strong.

4 × 100m relay, women former GDR
1985, 41.37secs

This is a very open contest, as last year's World Championships showed when the Bahamas, to everyone's surprise, won gold, with the USA languishing in fourth. The Americans should do better this time, and the Jamaicans and French also have a chance. Great Britain will do well to reach the final.

4 × 400m relay, men
USA
1998, 2mins 54.20secs,

With Michael Johnson in their line-up, the USA look irresistible. Britain will be hoping Iwan Thomas and Mark Richardson can keep them in contention and a silver medal is possible. Other challengers will be Jamaica, Brazil and Poland, who were a surprise second at last year's World Championships.

4 × 400m relay, women
USSR
1988, 3mins 15.17secs,

This should be a battle between the Russians and the Americans, with Germany an outside bet. Great Britain, with Katherine Merry in the team, should make the final, but that could be the best they achieve.

20km and 50km walk, men/10km walk, women

There are no official world records for the walk. The IAAF simply list the best times in each area of the world. Even more so than the marathon, the walks are very difficult to predict, but in the men's 20km walk look out for Julio Rene Martinez of Guadeloupe, the fastest walker in 1999. In the men's 50km event watch Segey Korepanov of Kazakhstan, and in the women's 10km event Nadezhda Ryashkina is a favourite to win.

DID YOU **KNOW?**

- In 1904 in St Louis, American Fred Lorz won the marathon but admitted later that he had hitched a ride in a car for 11 miles. He claimed afterwards it was a joke, but not many people laughed.

- In 1932, Polish sprinter Stella Walsh took the gold in the women's 100m. It was not until 'her' death in 1980 that it was discovered she was actually a man. Worried by the number of men passing themselves off as women, sex testing was introduced in 1968. A number of competitors mysteriously stopped entering competitions.

- In 1952, Czech runner Emil Zatopek completed an amazing triple, the 5000m, the 10,000m and the marathon – a race he had never run before.

- In the early modern Olympics, one of the field events was the tug of war. In 1908 Great Britain won it, with a team made up of members of the City of London police force.

- In 1924, 'Flying Finn' Paavo Nurmi won five gold medals, including the 1500m and the 5000m, which he won within an hour of each other.

BRITISH MEDAL COUNT

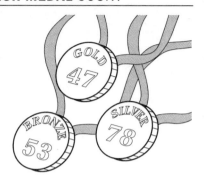

Badminton

16 – 23 September, Ross Pavilion

Ask people what the fastest racket sport in the world is and it is likely that most would say tennis or squash. Very few would say badminton, but they would be right. A shuttlecock, struck by a top professional with a modern racket, can travel at 200mph. Not bad for a piece of equipment made from sticking goose feathers into a piece of cork. However, the damage does take its toll on the shuttle, or 'bird', as it is known, and it can only last two games before being replaced.

Badminton is extremely demanding. The shuttle travels so fast that players have to possess lightning reflexes to keep it in play, together with superb stamina. Top players have been known to cover up to four miles in a single match. Unlike in tennis, where the flight and bounce of a ball can be predicted, the strange shape and material of the shuttle makes it difficult to predict how it will behave in flight. Therefore players must be extremely agile and light on their feet to counter this problem. Rallies last for much longer than tennis – about ten shots more on average – and the bird is in play for roughly double the time. So those who dismiss it as a game involving delicate pats back and forth over a net could not be more wrong.

Part of badminton's genteel image stems from the fact that it used to be a game played only by the upper classes. The sport derived from an Indian game, Poona, picked up by British army officers stationed in India, which gradually made its way back to these shores. The name changed when the Duke of Beaufort introduced the game at his country estate in Gloucestershire, called Badminton House. However, the game did not last long as the preserve of the English aristocracy, as the Chinese and Indonesians began to show their skill at the sport in the middle part of the last century. These two countries, together with Korea, now totally dominate the sport and all three are intense rivals. Only rarely do athletes from other nations manage to break this dominance.

WHAT TO **WATCH**

Badminton is similar to tennis, in that the court possesses tramlines acting as boundaries and a net, which is 59 inches high. Like tennis, Olympic badminton comprises five events – men's singles and doubles, women's singles and doubles, and mixed doubles, which was introduced at the last Games in Atlanta. In singles, the players try to make their opponent move across the whole court, measuring 44 feet by 17 feet, forcing them out of position in order to set up the winning shot. In doubles, where the court is three feet wider, most teams try to whip the ball low across the net so that the opposition can only keep the shuttle in play by lobbing it back high over the net, so setting up a smash shot. When attacking, one player stands at the net while the other remains at the back anticipating a smash. When defending, both players remain at the back of the court. This can lead to drop shots being used to try and defeat them. The players are so agile that most points are won by forcing opponents to make errors, such as hitting the net or hitting the shuttle outside the court boundaries, rather than by hitting extravagant winners.

WHAT ARE THE **RULES?**

A badminton match is the best of three games, so the first player or team to win two games takes the match. A game, in the doubles and men's singles, is won by being the first to reach 15 points, and two points clear. In women's singles, the first player to 11 points wins, though again they must be two points clear. If a match reaches 14 points all (10 points all for women) then the players can choose to 'set', which means the first person or team to reach 17 wins the game (13 for women's singles.) If the players choose not to 'set' then the game finishes at the usual point. Points can only be scored on a serve, so the receiving side solely seeks to win the right to serve.

Serving must be done from below the waist with the racket head below the server's hand and with part of both feet on the ground. The rules on serving differ between singles and doubles. In singles, the server must stand on the left-hand side of the court if their points total is an odd number, or right-hand portion if their score is nil or even. In doubles play, the player who serves first must do so from the right-hand portion of the court and swaps each time their side wins a rally. Should the rally be lost then the shuttle passes to the other side and the server launches the shuttle from the opposite side from where the last serve was played.

A rally is won when the shuttle touches the floor on the opposition's side of the net or if the shuttle is not kept in play.

Other major rules include:

- A shuttle landing on the line is considered in bounds.

- If the shuttle gets caught in the net during play then a 'let' is called and the rally is replayed, unless it occurs on a serve, in which case a fault is called.

- A player may let their racket go over the opposing side of the net during the follow-through on a shot.

- A shuttle may clip the net on a serve as long as it lands in the opposing side of the court.

WHO WILL **WIN?**

The game has traditionally been dominated by the Asian nations. Athletes from those countries picked up 14 of the 15 medals on offer four years ago in Atlanta, and the Chinese and Indonesians will be hoping to emulate that feat. The game is so popular in these countries that it is difficult to predict who will win the men's singles crown, but look out for China's Sun Jun and Indonesia's Budi Santoso. Denmark's Peter Grade Christiansen may provide Europe's best chance.

Britain's best medal hopes lay in the doubles events and both involve Simon Archer. With partner Nathan Robertson in the men's event, both will be hoping to better their bronze medals in the recent World Championships. Archer's best chance may be in the mixed doubles, with his partner Jo Goode, a pairing which won the silver medal at the World Championships. In the women's singles, Wales' Kelly Morgan, the Commonwealth champion, will be hoping to perform as well as she did in the World Championships, when she reached the quarter-finals. The favourites for the women's gold include China's Ye Zhaoying and Gong Zichao, with another Dane, Camilla Martin, flying the flag for Europe.

DID YOU **KNOW?**

- Due to its popularity in Asia, badminton is the second largest participation sport in the world behind football.

- During the last two Olympics, badminton had the second-highest worldwide TV viewing figures compared to any other event.

- Badminton, for all its global popularity, did not become an Olympic sport until 1992, despite being tested as a demonstration sport as far back as 1972.

- The fastest smash ever recorded was struck by Britain's Simon Archer, and was clocked at 260 kilometres per hour.

JARGON BUSTER

Alley: A 1½-foot by 2-foot extension of the court on both sides for doubles play.

Carry: An illegal shot, also called a sling or throw, in which the shuttle is caught and held on the racket and then fired like a sling shot from the strings.

Clear: A shot hit deep to the opponent's back boundary line. The 'high clear' is a high defensive shot, while the 'attacking clear' is flat and used offensively.

Drive: A fast and low horizontal shot over the net.

Drop: A shot hit softly and with finesse to fall rapidly and close to the net on the opponent's side.

Flick: A quick wrist and forearm rotation that surprises an opponent by changing an apparently soft shot into a faster passing one. Used primarily on the serve and at the net.

Hairpin net shot: Shot made from close to the floor and very close to the net in which the shuttle rises, barely clears the net, and then drops sharply down on the other side. The shuttle's flight approximates to the shape of a hairpin.

Kill: A fast, downward shot that cannot be returned. Also known as a 'putaway'.

Push shot: A gentle shot played by pushing the shuttle with little wrist motion, usually from the net or midcourt to the opponent's midcourt.

Wood shot: A shot that results when the base of the shuttle is hit by the frame of the racket. Once illegal, the shot was legalized in 1963.

Baseball

17 – 27 September, Olympic Park Baseball Stadium and
Blacktown Olympic Centre

For the first time in Olympic history, professional players will
be able to play for their respective countries at baseball.
This new ruling should give the United States a chance to
make up for all the defeats suffered in this competition at
the hands of arch-rivals Cuba, losses which still smart with
many Americans. The sport was accepted into the Olympics
in 1992, after being tested seven times since 1912 as a
demonstration sport. Both times the gold medal has gone to
Cuba while the US, fielding a team of amateurs and college
kids, have seen their pride crushed. Now, although the most
well-known Major League stars will not be appearing because
the tournament coincides with the close of the baseball
season, the USA will be able to field a much stronger side
than before, filled with up-and-coming professionals.

The game is seen around the globe primarily as an
American pastime and is part of American culture, to the
extent that the word 'Ruthian', named after the legendary
player Babe Ruth, is now in the American dictionary and
means 'an act of mammoth proportions'. However, baseball almost certainly derived from rounders and that

quintessentially English game, cricket. Some historians even credit the ancient Egyptians with the invention of the game. For Americans, though, baseball began in 1846 when the New York Nine met the bizarrely named Knickerbockers in Hoboken, New Jersey, and since then the game has become big business. It is now played in 120 countries and players of varied nationalities play in the American Major League.

WHAT TO **WATCH**

Eight teams will compete in the Games; Australia qualify as hosts, while the other seven reached the Games through a series of regional qualifiers. Each side will play each other once and the top four will advance to the semi-finals. The first-placed side will play the fourth, and the second plays the third. The winners contest the final, while the losers play off for the bronze medal.

The game is exactly the same as the professional sport, except that the use of aluminium bats is permitted in Sydney. In the Major League, only wooden bats can be used, since aluminium can give the batter extra power in the shot. 'Home runs' are the most spectacular part of the sport, where the ball is hit out of the playing area and the batter can run around all the bases without hindrance. Pitchers attempt to avoid such a result with a wide range of throws ('pitches'), such as curveballs, in order to prevent the batter hitting the ball at all and 'strike' him out. Some pitchers can throw the ball at speeds of more than 100mph.

WHAT ARE THE **RULES?**

The game is played between two sides over the course of nine innings. Each side takes a turn batting and fielding – an innings is closed when three of the batting side are out. After nine innings, if the scores are level, extra innings are played until one team gains a lead. Teams score a run when a batter reaches home base after advancing around all three bases, which are around 90 feet apart and form a diamond shape. The batter must reach first base before a fielder touches the base plate while holding the ball or catches the ball before it bounces. Home runs are usually hit over the outfield fence allowing the batter, and all those already at a base, to run home immediately. Most runs, however, are scored by advancing round the bases in turn. Other than striking the ball, a batter can reach first base if the opposing pitcher throws four 'balls' – pitches the umpire rules cannot be hit – or if he is hit on the body by a pitch.

Runners can only run to a next base if there is no other baserunner already occupying it. If, when running between the bases, a fielder with the ball tags them, then they are out.

A batter can be out in three ways:

- If a pitcher defeats him with three legitimate pitches – called a 'strikeout'.

- If the ball is hit to an infielder who gets the ball to first base before the batter reaches it.

- If the ball is hit in the air and caught.

The game has a number of small, but important rules, that those not familiar with the game need to know:

- A foul ball is called when the batter strikes the ball beyond the two 'foul lines' (the boundaries of the pitch). It counts as a strike until the batter has two strikes against him. A foul ball never counts as a third strike. However, he can be caught off a ball that is going to land in the 'foul' area (out of bounds).

- Even if a fielder catches the ball, baserunners can still try to advance to the next base. The ball must have been caught, though. If the batter strays from his base before then, then he will be out if the catching fielder gets the ball to his base before he returns.

- A baserunner can be tagged if he runs or slides past second or third base. He cannot be tagged if he overshoots first base.

- A baserunner can attempt to advance to another base at any time the ball is in play as long as the batter has not hit it. This is known as 'stealing'.

WHO WILL **WIN?**

Unsurprisingly, Britain failed to qualify for the Games. For everyone, the Cubans will be the team to beat. They did not lose a tournament between 1974 and 1997, when Japan finally defeated them in the Intercontinental Cup. However, the reigning champions showed they had recovered from that result by beating the Baltimore Orioles, a Major League side, 12–6 in an exhibition match in 1999. The side has played together for many years and, despite the defection of the odd star player to America to make big money, they have a tremendous spirit and will to win. The USA will hope to seriously challenge them with the addition of a few minor stars to their team, though the days of fielding a basketball-style 'Dream Team', made up of the best professional players, in the Olympics are still a long way off. The Japanese always play well and will be looking for a medal, as will the hosts, Australia, whose nascent baseball team have surprised everyone recently by their performances. With the help of home support, they could be the surprise team of the competition. Europe's representatives are Italy and Holland but, really, the most they can expect is to avoid humiliation.

DID YOU **KNOW?**

- The American, Mark McGwire, who recently smashed the record for the number of home runs scored in a single season, played as an amateur for his country in the 1984 Los Angeles Olympics.

- In the 1996 Olympic Games, Cuba's Orestes Kindelan hit a 521-foot home run, the longest home run in the history of the Atlanta-Fulton County Stadium, the home of the Major League side, the Atlanta Braves. In all, Kindelan struck nine home runs in nine games.

- The holder of the world record for the most home runs ever struck is not an American. In fact, it is Sadaharu Oh of Japan, who hit 868 home runs during a hugely successful career.

Basketball

16 September – 1 October, Sydney SuperDome

Since 1992, when the decision was taken to allow professionals to participate, Olympic men's basketball has been totally dominated by the USA. In that year, the so-called 'Dream Team' featured some of the highest-paid and best-known athletes on the planet, including Michael Jordan and Magic Johnson. That decision, continued in 1996 in Atlanta, is likely to extend to Sydney, where the other nations will probably find themselves competing for the silver and bronze medals, while the USA, with players like Gary Payton and Jason Kidd, should find it easy.

It has nearly always been this way. The sport arrived as an Olympic event in 1936 and for the next 36 years the top prize was won by the Americans, until 1972. Those Games, held in Munich, provided one of the Games' most controversial moments. In the final, the USA met the Soviet Union in a clash of the superpowers. With six seconds to play the Soviets led 49–48, until Doug Collins of the USA managed to give his side a one-point lead by sinking two free throws after being fouled. The horn sounded for the end of the game but the Russians alleged they had called a timeout just before Collins' second free throw, thus stopping the clock. An order was given for the clock to be reset with three seconds remaining, during which a long Russian throw failed to find the basket and the USA celebrated once more. Unfortunately, the clock was still being reset when the long throw was made and chaos reigned. The President of basketball's international ruling body (FIBA) stepped in and ordered the clock to be reset again. This time a long pass found Aleksander Belov, who nipped in to score the winning basket just before the final whistle, ending the USA's 62-game winning streak. A protest was lodged by the Americans, but was dismissed at a later hearing by three members of a five-man jury. Whether the nationalities of those three arbiters – Cuban, Polish and Hungarian – had anything to do with it is another matter. The Americans refused to accept their silver medals and what happened still hurts in many quarters.

The Soviets also took gold in 1980, following the American boycott of the Games in Russia, and then beat the Americans in the semi-finals of 1988 – the last time the game was played by amateurs at the Olympics. Now it is highly unlikely that anyone will get close enough to the USA to provide as dramatic a finale as that of 1972.

WHAT TO **WATCH**

Some of the world's best athletes will be on show in Sydney. No other sport mixes agility, pace, stamina, strength and versatility in quite the same fashion. The best players must be able to jump terrific heights, run at speed while controlling the ball, change direction at an instant, while having a 7-foot giant waving their arms in front of them, trying to harass them off the ball. The size and strength of the best Americans allow them to advance down the field at frightening speeds and score from almost any position. From under the basket they are superb, capable of jumping, twisting and then slamming the ball home for a score. Sydney should be an exhibition of the game's finer arts. Other teams will probably be unable to match the Americans under the basket and will attempt to launch long-distance shots. This is a risky strategy – the ball often bounces off the rim – but spectacular when it comes off.

WHAT ARE THE **RULES?**

Basketball is played between two teams of five players each. In the Olympics, the game consists of two 20-minute halves. The game stops whenever the referee blows his whistle to indicate a dead ball. If the score is tied at the end of the game, an extra five minutes 'overtime' is played.

Most baskets are worth two points, but a longer shot from behind an arced line 6.25 metres from the basket scores three. Once a basket is scored, the ball passes to the opposition who start play by passing the ball from an out-of-bounds position at the end of the court. They have 10 seconds in which to cross the halfway line, otherwise the ball is given back to the opposition who pass the ball from behind their side of the centre line. In possession, a side has 30 seconds to make a shot.

Basketball is supposed to be a non-contact sport, but in fact is one of the most physical games around. However, referees will penalize players who bump, barge and shove an opponent and award the fouled player free throws, worth one point each. If a player is fouled while trying to score a two-point shot, two free throws are awarded; if they are attempting a three-point score, then three throws are given. If a team is punished for seven fouls in one half, then for the rest of that half, a free throw is awarded for any foul, regardless of whether the player was trying to shoot. Players can, however, steal the ball out of the hands of their opponents as long as they do not make contact with the player himself.

Dribbling the ball can be done with either hand, but not both at the same time. A dribble stops when the player stops bouncing the ball and takes it in both hands – he or she may not then resume a dribble and must pass or shoot. While standing with the ball a player must keep one foot fixed to the floor, but can move the other. The player has five seconds to pass or shoot before the referee blows up and awards the ball to the other side. However, there is one exception. When going for the basket a player can take two steps after dribbling before shooting.

Other rules include:

- If a foul is committed in a situation where a player is not shooting, then the opposition takes the ball out of bounds at the nearest spot to where the foul occurred.

- The boundary line is considered out of bounds.

- The 30-second clock counting down the time a team has to shoot does not restart when the attacking side retains possession after a defensive player has touched the ball.

- Goal-tending, where a player puts a hand into the basket rim to stop the ball going in or palms it away when the shot is on a downward arc, is not allowed and the basket is awarded.

- A basket scored as playing time ends counts as long as the ball was in the air when time ran out.

The Olympic tournament is seeded according to how the teams fared in the 1998 World Championships and the qualification rounds for the Games. The 12 qualifiers are put into two groups of six and each team plays each other within their group. The top four teams in each group advance to the quarter-finals where the tournament turns into a straight knock-out competition. The losing semi-finalists play-off for the bronze medal.

WHO WILL **WIN?**

In short, the USA. Britain did not qualify, while the best European hope lies with Yugoslavia. They won the World Championships – the US suffered from a lack of professionals and injuries – and should contest the final with the 'Dream Team'. The European champions, Italy, and runners-up, Lithuania, will also be competitive, as will the Australians, who have made great strides in recent times. Russia, Spain and France will be the other European contenders. It will be interesting to see how well Angola, the African qualifiers, compete.

The women's tournament should be much more open, though the USA will again be the favourites. The hosts will be hoping to improve on their bronze medal in Atlanta, though the Brazilians will push them hard. The main European challenge should come from Russia, with China, South Korea, Cuba and Canada the only other sides likely to make an impact.

DID YOU **KNOW?**

- The hoop is 18 inches in diameter, wide enough to fit two basketballs side by side.

- The first basketball competition in 1936 was an utter disaster. The rules precluded players over 6 feet 2 inches in height from taking part and the game was played outdoors. The final was played in torrential rain, on a clay court also used for tennis. As a result, the ball wouldn't bounce and only 27 points were scored in total.

- The most prolific Olympian in this sport, surprisingly, is not American. He is Oscar Schmidt from Brazil, who has played 38 games over the last five Olympics, scoring 1093 points.

- The women's competition has featured one of the tallest ever Olympians in the shape of Julijana Semenova, who was 7 feet 2 inches tall. She led Russia to the gold medal in 1976 and 1980.

Boxing

16 September – 1 October, Sydney Exhibition Centre

No other Olympic sport has quite the illustrious history of boxing, but this is a history also riddled with controversy. For many years, the judging of Olympic boxing bouts was ridiculous. There are countless tales of boxers who have clearly beaten their opponent, only for the judges to decide against them, voting on political rather than sporting grounds. One example among many was the experience of Roy Jones, a 19-year-old American. He was named the most outstanding boxer of the 1988 Games, yet didn't win a gold medal. In the light-middleweight final he easily beat his South Korean opponent, Park Si-Hun, yet lost the points decision when three judges voted for Park and only two for Jones. Perhaps this was not surprising given that the Games were being held in Seoul, the capital of South Korea. Even the President of the International Olympic Committee (IOC), Juan Antonio Samaranch, expressed his reservations and the scoring system was changed.

In Barcelona in 1992, an electronic scoring system was introduced, and improved for the 1996 Games in Atlanta. Under this system, each of the five judges is linked to a central computer. When a boxer lands a punch, the judge pushes that boxer's button. If two other judges hit that button then the punch is credited to the boxer's score. The boxer with the most counted pushes wins. This allows the governing body to study the judges' decisions, using a printout, and weed out the most incompetent or corrupt judges.

It is a shame that quirky judging decisions have marred much of Olympic boxing's history, because no other sport has been graced by so many glittering names. To list just a few: Muhammad Ali (or Cassius Clay as he was at the time), 'Smokin'' Joe Frazier, George Foreman, Lennox Lewis, Sugar Ray Leonard, Jeff Fenech, Ingemar Johansson and Evander Holyfield have all graced the Olympics before becoming some of the sport's biggest names in the professional arena. Who knows who may emerge from the Sydney Olympics?

Boxing dates back 5000 years, and was a part of the ancient Games, when contestants fought until one of them collapsed, was knocked out or simply gave up. Fighters wore leather thongs on their hands, which were replaced in the Roman era by gloves studded with spikes and nails to rough the opposition up and, in many cases, kill them. The sport died with the Roman empire and did not re-emerge until the seventeenth century in England, with bare-knuckle fighting. In the mid-1800s the sport was cleaned up by the Marquess of Queensbury who introduced a set of rules which are still in use today. These eliminated bare-knuckle fighting, wrestling, hugging and the beating of helpless opponents. Rounds were three minutes long, with a one-minute break, and boxers had to wear gloves. In 1896, the sport was deemed too 'ungentlemanly, dangerous and practised by the dregs of society' to warrant a place in the Athens Games of that year. In 1904, it debuted as a demonstration sport, gained official status at the 1908 Games in London, where Britain took all five gold medals, only to be dropped by the Swedes for the 1912 Games in Stockholm. However, in 1920 it was back for good and, bizarre judging decisions aside, the sport has not looked back since.

WHAT TO **WATCH**

All Olympic boxers are amateurs. In many ways, this allows spectators to see the sport in its purest form, untainted by the money and corruption that now dogs the professional sport. Because of its amateur status, all competitors must wear protective headgear, and referees are quick to step in and halt a bout if one boxer is clearly losing, usually to deliver a standing count of eight to allow the boxer to regain his composure, or to stop the fight if they believe the boxer is in danger. In general, the referees exercise much stricter control than in professional boxing, where financial interests and a wish to keep fans happy means referees are sometimes loath to step in and end a fight. In the Olympics, boxers must obey the referees' requests to stop or break or they will find themselves losing points, or being disqualified.

WHAT ARE THE **RULES?**

In Sydney, rather than the usual bouts of three three-minute rounds, fights will consist of four two-minute rounds. This has been introduced because doctors believe that fighters will suffer less punishment in two-minute rounds. There is an interval of one minute between each round.

To score a point, a fighter must land a clean punch, delivered with the knuckle area of the glove. The scoring areas are the head and the front and sides of the torso from the waist up. Blows to the arm or weak punches score no points.

Boxers score one point if three judges agree the punch was clean and forceful. If there is a flurry of punches, too quick to score electronically, the judges wait until the boxers have finished trading blows and give the point to the one they feel got the best of the exchange. At the end of the bout the boxer with the most points awarded by a majority of the judges is the winner. If the boxers are tied, then judges award the bout to the most attacking, stylish fighter.

If, during the fight, the boxer touches the canvas with any part of his body other than his feet, and if any part of his body is outside the ropes or if he is hanging helplessly from the ropes, he is considered 'down'. The referee begins a count of 10, which is also counted electronically, and if the boxer fails to recover before the end of the count, the bout is considered a knockout. A count can also be given to a boxer who is still on his feet whom the referee has judged unable to continue.

In amateur boxing, even if a boxer recovers immediately from being put down he must still take a mandatory count of eight while standing on his feet. The referee will then decide if the boxer is able to continue but can stop the bout if he feels the boxer is incapable of defending himself or is in danger. If a boxer receives three standing-eight counts in one round, or four in the whole fight, then he is judged to have lost the fight. The referee can also stop a fight if one boxer has been badly cut and has been deemed by a doctor as unfit to continue. The other boxer wins the fight in these two cases.

A boxer can only be 'saved by the bell' (which sounds to mark the end of a round) in the final round of a bout. In the other three rounds, the count continues after the bell. If both boxers go down then both receive a count, until one gets up.

If they are both counted out then the boxer with the most points wins. A bout can also end if the corner representing one boxer feels he is taking too much punishment and withdraws their fighter, known as 'throwing in the towel'.

Boxers can be penalized for a number of illegal activities, many of which are well known, such as hitting below the belt, holding, hitting with the palm of the glove and hitting an opponent on the back of the head. A caution is given when one of these fouls is committed, two cautions constitute a warning, and three cautions result in disqualification.

For the 2000 Games, there are 12 weight divisions, which are as follows, from the lightest upwards: Light Flyweight, Flyweight, Bantamweight, Featherweight, Lightweight, Light Welterweight, Welterweight, Light Middleweight, Middleweight, Light Heavyweight, Heavyweight, Super Heavyweight.

The boxers are drawn together in random pairs and fight in a knock-out tournament. The two semi-final winners compete for gold and silver, while both losers receive the bronze.

WHO WILL **WIN?**

At the time of press, qualifiers for the boxing competition had still to be determined. However, British boxers will be there and some will have a good chance of winning medals. Cuba is the team to watch as they have dominated the event in recent years, and in Felix Savion, they have the undisputed king of amateur boxing. He has won four World Championship heavyweight titles and if he wins in Sydney, it will be his third gold medal. Likewise, his compatriot Ariel Hernandez will be battling for his third straight gold in the middleweight division if he decides to compete. The USA are always strong having won 46 gold medals in 19 Olympics.

DID YOU **KNOW?**

- In Tokyo in 1964, Spanish flyweight Valentin Loren was banned for life when he punched a referee.

- In 1904, boxing was made a demonstration sport for the Games in St Louis, USA. The Americans won all the medals, not surprising since they were the only country that entered. Women's boxing was also a demonstration sport.

- In the ancient Games, a man named Melagomas used to force his opponents to withdraw and admit defeat without a single blow being exchanged, so intimidating was his presence.

- Beards are prohibited in Olympic boxing, and moustaches must not be longer than the upper lip.

- In the Tokyo Olympics, 'Smokin'' Joe Frazier won the super heavyweight gold despite fighting with a broken right hand.

BRITISH MEDAL COUNT

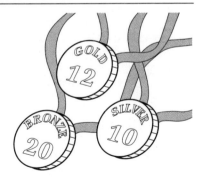

Canoe/Kayak

Slalom: 16 – 20 September, Penrith Lakes
Sprint: 26 – 28 September, Sydney International
Regatta Centre

There are two forms of canoe/kayak races. The sprint, held on flat water with competitors assigned to lanes, and the slalom, held on turbulent whitewater with paddlers going down a course of gates one at a time, racing against the clock. The difference between a canoe and a kayak is simple; a canoe is a closed boat paddled from a kneeling position with a single-bladed paddle, while a kayak is a closed boat paddled from a sitting position using a double-bladed paddle. Women compete only in kayaks. The sprint race first entered the Olympics as a medal sport in 1936, while the slalom first made an appearance in 1972, though it disappeared straight away and did not resurface until 1992 in Barcelona.

The competitors in the Sydney Games will be hoping the course is less exacting than the choppy waters of the Ocoee River in Atlanta, which many observers believed provided too much of a challenge. About 12 paddlers capsized during the event, far too many for a serious competition, though it provided the crowd with lots of excitement.

In an attempt to make the scoring system fairer, a new rule has been introduced into the canoeing event in Sydney

– one that will come as a major relief to all the participants. Instead of losing five seconds for grazing one of the gates in the slalom event – a massive penalty to pay in a sport where every second counts – only two seconds will be added to a competitor's time. One only needs to cite the example of Jon Lugbill in the 1992 Barcelona Olympics. The American had won the race with the fastest time and was poised to pick up the gold medal, only to lose out on any medal at all because he had skimmed the 23rd gate, something he did not realize he had done. Skimming a gate is now less likely to be the difference between greatness and mediocrity.

WHAT TO **WATCH**

The first point is that competitors don't row, they paddle. Unlike their rowing counterparts, canoe/kayak racers always face forwards in their boats. In total, there are 16 events in the Olympic competition, 12 of which are sprints on flatwater. In Sydney, the slalom events will be held on Penrith Lakes on an artificial 300-metre course, while the sprint events take place nearby at the Sydney International Regatta Centre, also the venue for the rowers.

Each of the events is known by a shorthand name, constructed from either a 'K' or a 'C' (for kayak or canoe) and a number, which refers to the number of paddlers in the boat, followed by the distance of the race. So, for example, the C1 500m on flatwater refers to the 500-metre sprint in a canoe with just one paddler on board. The K4 1000m for men, a sprint with four paddlers in the kayak, has the highest number of competitors on board.

The main difference between boats that race on flat water and whitewater is in their length. Flatwater boats are longer and sleeker and possess steering rudders, while whitewater boats are more compact to enable them to turn quickly around the gates on a slalom course. Canoes, in general, are larger and more difficult to control than kayaks, the stated reason for the lack of a women's canoe event.

WHAT ARE THE **RULES?**

Sprint

Sprint races are straight races to the line over either 500 or 1000 metres. The sprint is started by a starter's gun and ends when the bow of a boat crosses the line. This, apparently, stops racers capsizing their boat and lunging at the line with their bodies to win a close race. The boats race in nine-metre-wide lanes, but are forbidden from going within five metres of another boat in a different lane. This rule stops boats riding in the wash of other boats or being pulled along in broken water caused by another boat. This rule is taken very seriously, so much so that if a boat's wash goes into the path of another boat, the onus is on the latter boat to avoid it. Usually, an umpire will warn the offending boat through a megaphone first, but if it takes place again then disqualification is a possibility.

At Sydney, there will be three women's, and nine men's, sprints. The women will race in the 500m K1, K2 and K4. The men will compete in the 500m K1 and K2, the 1000m K1, K2 and K4, and the 500m and 1000m C1 and C2 races.

Among the rules are:

- If the paddlers capsize they can continue to race as long as they get back into their boat without anyone else's help.

- If an umpire has seen a rule being violated, he or she will raise a red flag at the race's end. If a white flag is waved then no violation has occurred and the result stands.

Teams are seeded (according to previous results) to distribute the favourites evenly, and placed in heats. The most successful boats advance through the competition to decide the medals.

Slalom

The slalom event is similar to skiing. Going down one at a time, the paddlers attempt to reach the bottom of the course as quickly as possible, while passing through gates without hitting any of them. As mentioned earlier, grazing a gate, which is made up of two poles suspended slightly above the water, with either the body, boat or paddle incurs a two-second time penalty. More seriously, if a paddler does not pass through a gate then they incur a 50-second penalty, which effectively means they are out of the competition. If a gate is missed the paddler can go back and attempt to pass through the gate again, but they may suffer the indignity of a subsequent paddler overtaking them on the course. Competitors tackle the course twice during both the heats and finals, with the times and penalties added together and converted into points. The paddler with the lowest points total wins.

Officials decide the gate sequence the day before the competition. Competitors are not allowed any trial runs. Their first attempt is, therefore, when the competition begins. Also at least six of the gates must be negotiated upstream, meaning that the paddler must battle against the whitewater to go through them. Competitors are provided with a diagram of the course which they must learn carefully – failure to do so can prove completely disastrous!

There are four slalom events made up of one women's race (the K1), and three men's races (the K1, C1 and the two-man C2). Each event involves qualification through heats followed by a final. The results of the qualification heats determine the order of the first run in the final, and the result of this first run determines the order of the second run with the last-placed paddler going first.

Other rules include:

- A judge's naked eye decides all rulings on gate penalties. No electronic equipment is used to detect if a gate has been grazed or skimmed.

- One judge watches each gate.

- Safety helmets and lifejackets must be approved by judges.

WHO WILL **WIN?**

British hopes are high after fantastic performances in the World Sprint Championships in Milan, Italy, last year, which acted as a qualifier to the 2000 Olympics. Britain secured places for seven athletes (five boats). Brothers Andrew and Steven Train got through in the C2 1000m event, while Ross Sabberton and Paul Darby-Dowman booked a place in the K2 1000m event. Also, look out for Ian Wynne in the K1 500m event and Tim Brabants in the K1 1000m event. The only woman's place went to Tricia Davey in the K1 500m event. John Anderson, the Performance Director at the British Canoeing Union, has high hopes for the sprint side. 'Over the past two seasons our sprint racing team has been going from strength to strength, culminating in the outstanding Olympic qualifications.'

However, in the sprint events, the nations to beat are Germany, Sweden and Russia, all traditionally strong in this sport. Individuals to take note of are Birgit Fischer of Germany, the top women's medal winner in Olympic history with a total of nine medals, and Norway's Knut Holman who will be looking to win both the 500m and 1000m men's K1 event.

Slalom

Like the sprint events, Britain had a fantastic time at the World Slalom Championships last year in Le Seu d'Urgell in Spain, which again acted as a qualifier for Sydney. Paul Ratcliffe won the men's K1 event, and will be hoping to repeat that performance in Sydney. He remains Britain's best hope of canoe/kayak gold. The formidable pairing of Nick Smith and Stuart Bowman will join him in the C2 event and Stuart McIntosh in the C1 class. Heather Corrie is Britain's only representative in the women's K1 event.

DID YOU **KNOW?**

- At the 1968 Olympics in Mexico, Anna Pfeffer of Hungary capsized in her kayak and had to be rescued by emergency boat. It did not affect her though, as 90 minutes later, she entered the K2 500m and won a silver medal.

- A kayak with four paddlers can generate enough speed to pull along a water skier.

- The slalom was removed from the Sydney Olympics programme, but reinstated when a deal was struck between a local council, the International Canoe Federation and the state government to build a whitewater course on Penrith Lakes.

- The course is a 300-metre channel between two ponds and drops five-and-a-half metres over its length. It is completely man-made, with six pumps lifting water from the bottom pond back to the top at a rate of 14 tonnes per second.

JARGON BUSTER

Blade: The wide, flat area of a paddle, used for propulsion.

Broach: Occurs when a canoe or kayak becomes caught in the current against an obstruction and turns sideways.

Chute: An area where the river's flow is suddenly constricted, compressing and amplifying the current's energy into a narrow tongue of water.

Eddy: Area behind or downstream of an obstruction in the main current, where water swirls in a direction different to that of the main flow, usually upstream.

Eskimo roll: A self-rescue technique used to right an overturned boat in the water without leaving it.

Fifted gate: Slang for missing a gate or passing through a gate while rolling or underwater, or any other infraction resulting in a 50-point penalty.

Hydraulic: Water formation following a sudden drop in the riverbed, or drop over an obstruction, which creates a powerful circulating force at the base of the drop. Also called a hole or reversal.

Touch: Penalty for touching a gate with the body, paddle or boat during whitewater competition.

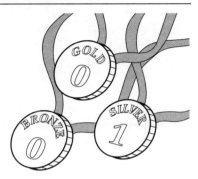

Cycling

Track: 16 – 21 September, Dunc Gray Velodrome
Road: 26 – 30 September, Road Cycling Course
Mountain Bike: 23 – 24 September, Fairfield City Farm

Cycling has provided the Olympics with some of its most stirring moments over the past century. For British fans, Chris Boardman's exhilarating gold medal at the 1992 Games in Barcelona in the individual pursuit was the most memorable, riding a space-age bike that weighed about seven pounds – but cost about £30,000. It gave British cycling an immense boost, which is reflected in the number of medal hopes.

Over the past century the sport has evolved considerably, with new technologies allowing riders to go faster and faster. Cycling has now branched out into three different disciplines – road, track and the baby of the group, mountain biking. In all, there will be 18 medal events at the 2000 Games – 12 on the track, four on the road and two for mountain bikes.

The sport first appeared in the first modern Games in 1896, and was swiftly identified as one of the most gruelling events. The first road course covered 87 kilometres, which, considering some of the distances to have appeared in subsequent years, was a pleasurable jaunt. The longest, by some distance, was at the 1912 Stockholm Games where the cyclists were required to cycle an amazing 199 miles, starting at 2 a.m. Needless to say, not all those who started finished the race, including the Swedish rider Karl Landsberg, who, shortly after starting, was struck by a motor vehicle and dragged along behind it for a couple of hundred yards.

Europe has traditionally dominated the road race events, not surprising given the history of events like the Tour de France, with Italy, France and Sweden among the most successful teams. In 1960, a Danish cyclist, Knut Jensen, died when the race was held in Rome in oppressive heat. The rider caught sunstroke, fell and suffered a fractured skull in the process. An autopsy revealed traces of a blood-circulation stimulant in his body, which highlights one of the problems of modern cycling, particularly long-distance road races – performance-enhancing drugs. The International Cycling Union is desperately attempting to clean up the sport after a series of doping scandals brought its credibility into question. Many of the top names in the sport have been tarnished and it could be a number of years before the problem is brought under control.

Track cycling also entered the Olympics in 1896, though many of the events of that year have disappeared. They were the one-lap race, 100-kilometre track race and a 12-hour endurance ride, which only two competitors completed. Women got their own track events in 1988 which have expanded over the years. However, mountain biking did not achieve Olympic status until four years ago. Instead of competing on flat surfaces, some cyclists sought the challenge of riding over dirt, hills and gullies. The first mass-produced bike to able to achieve this became available in 1981 and the popularity of the bike has grown massively. A World Cup series was introduced in 1991, which took the sport out of the USA (where it originated) and over to Europe before it gained Olympic status in Atlanta. It looks as if it is here to stay.

WHAT TO **WATCH**

There are three different types of cycling events requiring different skills, strengths and equipment. Most of the events take place on the track, a 250-metre indoor arena in which the atmosphere can be overwhelming. This will host individual and team events, sprint and endurance races.

Four of the track races are events for both men and women – the time trial, sprint, individual pursuit and a points race. Only the men compete in the team pursuit, madison, keirin and the Olympic sprint (see below for all events). Track cyclists need to be powerful and muscular to sprint at high speeds. They also use specially designed bikes and aerodynamic outfits to minimize wind resistance as they fly round the track at high speeds.

Road racers, because they cycle for longer distances, need great stamina. The ability to control breathing is vital in order to survive the punishing distances. Road cyclists are often smaller than their track counterparts – the average height is around 5 feet 8 inches, meaning they have less weight to carry.

Mountain biking can be a lottery, because the rough terrain means mechanical failure is always an issue. The bikes are fitted with heavy-duty suspension to cope with the trails the races are held on. Cyclists need to be strong to cope with the harsh, unpredictable courses they encounter and need bravery to attack obstacles at high speed. Most of all, they need luck on their side.

WHAT ARE THE **RULES?**

Here is a guide to each of the 11 different cycling events:

TRACK

Time Trial

The men compete over four laps (1km) while the women race over two (500m). Cyclists race one at a time and the rider with the fastest time wins the gold. It is a pure test of stamina and speed.

Sprint

For both men and women this is a three-lap race, though only the last 200 metres are timed. Two cyclists race head-to-head and aim to be the first to cross the finishing line. Riders will spend the opening laps jockeying for position, riding very slowly, sometimes even coming to a complete, though temporary standstill since they want to save all their energy for the final sprint. Riders must keep moving on the first lap at no slower than walking pace, but for the next two laps anything goes, including some explosive bursts of sprinting. Several heats determine the top two riders who then compete for the gold.

Individual Pursuit

The race in which Britain's Chris Boardman won his gold in 1992. Two riders start on opposite sides of the track and attempt to catch each other, or if not, clock the fastest time. The race is 4km for the men, 3km for the women. The first round is made up of heats in which only time counts, with the four best going through to the semi-finals. At the outset of the race, cyclists are held in their blocks for 50 seconds before the signal is given to start. Tactically, most riders will hug the inside line all around the track.

Team Pursuit

This is a four-man version of the individual pursuit and is for the men only. Teams will save energy by riding wheel-to-wheel directly behind one another, and take turns to lead while the other team members rest by riding in the slipstream. The third rider is the pivotal team member because in order to win, he must draw level with his opposite number. If no one is caught, then the times of both third riders are compared and the fastest wins.

Points Race

The object of this race is to gain the most points over one 40km race (25km for women). The race begins with a mass flying start and riders then fight for the point-scoring positions. The first four riders who cross the finishing line every tenth lap score points – five for first, three for second, two for third and one for fourth. In the final sprint to the line, points count double. Following the race's completion, the winner is the rider who has lapped the field, meaning they caught up with, and overtook, the last-placed rider. If more than one rider laps the field, a common occurrence, the winner is the one with the most points.

Madison

This men-only race bears a similarity to the points race. It was first contested at Madison Square Gardens, New York, hence the name. It begins with a mass start and is a sort of relay involving two riders per team who try to accumulate points by winning sprints throughout the race. They change over by gripping hands with one another, the rider who has just raced propelling his partner into the race. While not racing, the partner slowly circles the top of the track waiting to re-enter. The race is over 240 laps, with a sprint every 20 laps. The points are the same as for the points race.

Keirin

This race makes its Olympic debut in Sydney, having begun as a betting race in 1940s Japan. It takes place over eight laps, with competitors riding behind a motorbike for the first five-and-a-half laps, which gradually increases its speed from 25kph to 45kph before leaving the track. The race is then a sprint for the finish.

Olympic Sprint

Another Olympic debut. It is a men's event involving two teams of three riders. The teams start on opposite sides of the track and sprint for three laps. Each team member leads his team for one lap. The first rider is usually a quick sprinter, the second a long-distance sprinter and the third a kilometre rider. The team finishes when the third rider crosses the line and the fastest time wins. The eight fastest times make the quarter-finals and then the race competition becomes a straight knockout to decide the medals.

ROAD

Road Race

This is cycling's equivalent of the marathon. It begins with a mass start and the aim is to simply cross the finishing line first. The men's race is over 234 kilometres, while the women compete over 126 kilometres. Put simply, the race is a gruelling test of endurance and stamina with liquid and food available from stations along the course. Riders who are lapped are required to leave the course unless they are on the final lap. Cyclists can legally travel in each other's slipstream, allowing them to conserve energy.

Time Trial
Similar to the track time trial, except over a much longer course. Men compete over 45.8 kilometres while women tackle 31.2 kilometres. Riders set out one by one at 90-second intervals and are timed over the course. The best time wins. Riding in the slipstream of another rider is not allowed in this event. If one cyclist catches another he must pass leaving a two-metre gap between them.

MOUNTAIN BIKE

Men race over a distance of 40–50 kilometres, while the women compete over 30–40 kilometres. The exact distance is not decided upon until the night before the race, to take into account weather conditions.

Competitors start at the same time, complete a lap of a 1.8-kilometre start loop before heading out to the main course.

Unlike road and track cycling where riders can receive assistance for mechanical troubles, mountain bikers cannot. They carry their own repair kits and must see to every problem themselves. The Sydney course is a bush track of mainly rough terrain, featuring gullies and other obstacles. The first to reach the finishing line wins.

The bikes are much sturdier than in the road and track events. They are fitted with a front suspension similar to a motorbike, and often have shock absorbers at the rear. They have straight handlebars, powerful brakes and 24 gears.

WHO WILL **WIN?**

Not for the first time Britain's main hope of cycling gold rests with Chris Boardman. Now an experienced road racer, he is expected to win a medal in the road time trial, an event in which he won silver four years ago, and last year came third in the World Championships. Sydney is probably his last Olympics so he will be really motivated, but he will have to beat off strong challenges from current world champion, Jan Ullrich of Germany, Michael Andersson of Sweden, Raivis Belohvosciks of Latvia, Jens Voigt of Germany and Erik Dekker of the Netherlands. In the road race, some big names will be looking to grab the glory. American Lance Armstrong, winner of the 1999 Tour de France, will be a favourite, as will Frenchman Laurent Jalabert. The crowd's favourite will be Australian rider Stuart O'Grady, who should do very well.

On the track, the British team has real medal hopes in the Olympic Sprint event. Chris Hoy, Craig Maclean and Jason Queally are the 1999 World Cup champions, European champions and won silver at last year's World Championships. The main threat to them comes from Spain, Greece, Italy and France. Jason Queally also goes in the kilometre time trial. He came fifth in the World Championships, just hours after being knocked off his bike while cycling on the road. His strongest competition comes from Stefan Nimke of Germany, Jose Escuredo of Spain and Dimitris Georgialis of Greece.

We also have outside chances of a medal in the team pursuit and the women's individual pursuit. In the former, British men have had a string of top ten finishes in World Cup competitions, but will need to be at their best to contend with the Ukraine, Italy, Russia, France and Germany. In the latter, Yvonne McGregor will be hoping for a medal against rivals Lucy Sharman of Australia, Judith Arnt of Germany, France's Marion Clignet and Rasa Nazeikyte of Lithuania.

Favourites are hard to name in the mountain biking. Britain's greatest hope is Caroline Alexander who had second- and fourth-place finishes in last year's World Cup series. Other favourites include Alison Sydor of Canada, Alison Dunlap of the USA and Gunn-Rita Dahle of Norway. In the men's event, world number one Miguel Martinez of France is favourite to take gold.

DID YOU **KNOW?**

- In 1920 Henry Kaltenbrun of South Africa believed he had won the road race when he crossed the line first. However, it transpired that Sweden's Harry Stenqvist had been held up for four minutes at one of the six railway crossings on the course. After taking this stop into account it was discovered the Swede had a better time and he was awarded gold.

- During a men's sprint on the track in 1964, Italy's Giovanni Pettenella and France's Pierre Trentin stood still on the track for 21 minutes and 57 seconds, an Olympic record.

- Riding in the slipstream of another rider is not always appreciated. In 1972, the Dutch team unofficially rode together, protecting the eventual winner Henni Kuiper all the way. One rival became so incensed at what was happening that he tried to punch a member of the Dutch team in the face while in the saddle. Asked why they rode so selflessly for Kuiper, a Dutch rider said it was because 'he is one of the nicest blokes around'.

Bonk: A sudden loss of strength as the result of physical exhaustion. Also known as 'hitting the wall'.

Brain bucket: Helmet.

Bunny hop: An acrobatic manoeuvre in which the rider 'hops' the bike over obstacles on a flat surface with nothing to jump off.

Chain ring tattoo: The dotted-line scar that bikers receive after gouging a shin on the chain ring.

Death cookies: Fist-sized rocks found along the course.

Fat tyre: Commonly accepted term for the mountain bike and everything associated with it.

Granny gear: The third and smallest chain ring on a mountain bike, combined with the biggest rear cassette ring. This is the lowest gear, used for extremely steep climbs.

Potato chip: A tweaked wheel rim.

Rig: An affectionate term for one's bike.

Single track: A path or trail wide enough for only one rider at a time.

Snakebite: The most common type of flat tyre, caused by hitting an obstacle so hard that the inner tube is pinched against the rim. This results in a double puncture that resembles two fang holes.

Switchback: A tight, zigzag turn on the face of the mountain, negotiated either uphill or downhill.

Travel: A measurement of the amount of suspension on a bike. Some downhill bikes have up to 10 inches of travel.

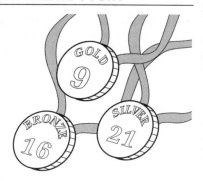

Diving

22 – 30 September, Sydney International Aquatic Centre

Diving is one of the most thrilling and eagerly anticipated Olympic sports, and in Sydney it has been given an extra twist to make it even more exciting. For the first time, synchronized diving will be part of the event. Two divers will leap side by side from both the 10-metre fixed platform and the three-metre springboard, the two traditional diving heights for men and women. Divers will attempt to mirror each other's speed along the board, the height of the jump, their rotation through the air and entry into the water. It promises to be a riveting addition to the Olympic schedule.

The introduction of synchronized diving reflects the growing popularity of the sport. Over the years it has provided the Olympics with some of its most memorable moments, in particular the feats of American diver, Greg Louganis, probably the best of all-time. Many remember the event in Seoul in 1988 when Louganis smashed his head on the springboard while attempting an elaborate dive. Unperturbed, he returned with stitches in his head to claim gold in both men's events.

Diving surfaced as a competitive sport towards the end of the nineteenth century. Competitions were arranged in

Britain that involved divers jumping headfirst into ponds. Luckily, the sport was combined with 'fancy diving', a phrase coined to describe the practice of performing acrobatics over water by Swedish and German gymnasts. The result is the sport we know today.

In 1904, platform diving (from a fixed structure) made its first appearance in the Games, and was followed four years later by springboard diving. Women got their chance to join in the fun in 1912, and eight years later had their own springboard competition. Over the years, dives have become increasingly difficult and elaborate, to the appreciation of ever-growing crowds.

It takes a huge amount of skill to be a diver, and even greater amounts of courage. Most of us know what it is like to tremble on top of a low diving board before reluctantly belly-flopping into the pool, but divers know that if they get a dive wrong it can be tremendously painful. The force of hitting the water at 35mph can be massive and injury is a real problem. The highest platform is about the size of a three-storey building. It can be an extremely lonely place to be, knowing that the difference between the perfect dive and a hideous flop is marginal.

WHAT TO **WATCH**

Unfortunately, diving comes tied up with a great deal of jargon that many people find hard to follow. Many of us switch off when commentators mention a reverse 2½ pike or a 3½ somersault tuck and prefer to watch the dives in a state of blissful ignorance. To put it simply though, there are six different groups of dives – though only five in the springboard competition – which are:

1. Forwards – The diver jumps head first off the board.

2. Backwards – This dive is executed when a diver takes off with their back to the water so they are facing backwards off the board, but still jump head first. The diver's rotation must be away from the board.

3. Reverse – The diver is facing forwards and then rotates back towards the board. Also referred to as a 'gainer'.

4. Inwards – The diver begins a dive with their back towards the water. Rotation on this dive occurs toward the board. Sometimes also referred to as a cut-away.

5. Twist – This requires a twisting motion off the board to get into position for any of the four dives above.

6. Armstand – This only takes place in platform diving. The diver begins his dive by performing a handstand on the edge of the platform.

Once airborne, the diver must keep their toes pointed while assuming one of four positions:

- Straight – arms and body fully extended, and feet together.

- Pike – body bent at the waist, but the legs stay straight.

- Tuck – the body is curled with knees and thighs brought up to the chest.

- Free – combining any two positions with a twist.

WHAT ARE THE **RULES?**

Divers will attempt dives with the highest degree of difficulty in order to score higher points. For example, a forward $2\frac{1}{2}$

somersault pike from the springboard carries a degree of difficulty of 2.4, while a reverse 3½ somersault tuck from the platform carries a rating of 3.4. Dives range between 1.3 and 3.6 in difficulty, and a formula allows judges to allocate a degree of difficulty to dives created by the divers themselves.

The degree of difficulty is vital because it plays a part in the divers' score. Following each dive, each of the five judges award a score between zero and 10, increasing in half-point increments. The highest and lowest of the scores are dropped (to eliminate judging bias) and the remaining five are added together. This total is multiplied by the degree of difficulty, and that total is then multiplied by 0.6 to produce a final score. The 0.6 is added to the mix because in the past only three judges used to score divers rather than five, so it allows modern dives to be compared with those in past Games.

To produce a score, judges break the dive down into different components and look for:

- A smooth approach along the board or platform.

- A controlled and balanced takeoff.

- Good height off the board or platform, which gives the diver more time to execute the dive.

- A well-executed dive. This is the most important aspect. The judges will look at body positioning, grace and technique.

- The entry into the water, which should create as little splash, and be as straight, as possible. In recent times this has become an extremely important component.

Diving has a number of other rules, including:

- No later than 24 hours before the event, divers must provide a list of all the dives they intend to do during the competition. Any dives other than the ones provided will score no points.

- A dive performed in any position other than the one stated by the judges can score no more than two points from each judge.

- If a diver assumes partially the wrong position during a dive then no more than 4.5 points from each judge can be awarded.

- While executing a standing dive, as opposed to a dive performed after a run-up, a diver cannot bounce on a springboard or platform.

In Sydney, a preliminary round will cut the field to 18 for the semi-finals, with 12 advancing through to the final. The semi-final and final scores combined determine the final result, with the top three divers picking up the medals.

The synchronized diving event differs in the way it is judged. In all, it will have a panel of nine judges; five judge the synchronization, while four judge the execution of the dives, two watching each diver. The synchronization judges are simply looking to see how co-ordinated the divers are in approach, take-off, timing of movements in the air, similarity of entry angles and timing of entry.

The highest and lowest scores are then discarded and the final score is calculated in the same manner as with the other dives.

WHO WILL **WIN?**

In the past, the USA has dominated the event, winning 46 of the 75 gold medals ever awarded. But in recent years they appear to have been overtaken by the Chinese, who won three of the gold medals at Atlanta and are likely to do just as well in Sydney. They possess three of the favourites in Yu Zhuocheng, Sun Shuwei and Tian Lang, but will be pushed hard by Mexico's Fernando Platas and Germany's Andreas Wels. In the women's events, watch for Xiaoqlao Liang and Xue Sang of China, Canadian Myriam Boileau and Yulia Pakhalina of the Ukraine.

The synchronized event will almost certainly be won by either China, Germany, Mexico or the Ukraine, with the hosts, Australia, possessing an outside chance.

DID YOU **KNOW?**

- When the sport was introduced at the 1904 St Louis Games diving for distance was one of the events. The objective was to swim the farthest underwater. The problem was no one could see what was going on and it was extremely spectator unfriendly. It was dropped, never to return.

- At the 1920 Games, the competition was held in an old moat in Antwerp. The water was clammy, cold and black so divers could not see into what they were diving. Now pools must have a depth of at least 4.5 metres and the water is heated to a 'desirable' temperature.

- All modern diving arenas have technology to ripple the water for the benefit of divers. The 'ripple effect' means divers can ascertain how far they are from the water during a dive, and while turning over in the air it helps them differentiate water from sky.

- The sport can be very dangerous. In 1983 the Russian diver Sergei Shalbashivili was tragically killed when he hit his head against a concrete platform during a dive.

JARGON BUSTER

Approach: The forward steps taken by a diver towards the end of the board. This precedes the hurdle (see below) and the take-off and usually involves three or more steps.

Balk: A balk occurs when a diver initiates motion to begin a dive but discontinue s prior to leaving the diving board. A balk is declared by the referee and causes a deduction of two points per judge.

Entry: The point in a dive in which the diver makes contact with the water.

Hurdle: Just after the approach, the diver hops, or springs, to the end of the board, taking off from one foot and landing on two feet. The take-off occurs immediately after the hurdle.

Equestrian

Dressage: 23 September – 1 October, Equestrian Centre
Showjumping: 23 September – 1 October, Equestrian Centre
Three-Day Event: 16 – 22 September, Equestrian Centre

1999 was an awful year for equestrianism, with a bewildering series of fatal accidents in three-day events, including the death of the British rider, Polly Phillips. The deaths occurred when riders fell at fences during cross-country races and their horses tumbled on top of them. The equestrian authorities have been looking into the issue of safety and some workable solutions may be in place in Sydney.

It would be sad if the equestrian events were to be overshadowed by concerns over the rider's safety, because it is one of the most thrilling and unique sports in the Games. Made up of three disciplines, dressage, three-day eventing and showjumping, it is the only sport where man and animal work together and where older sportsmen and women can compete with youth and power. Age, guile and experience count for a great deal in equestrian events. Significantly, it is also the only truly open sport in the Olympics, with men and women competing side by side. In fact, in terms of the three-day event, the men, particularly in Europe, have a bit of catching up to do. In September 1999 at the European Championships, for the first time at a major eventing championship, three women stood on the podium to collect the medals, with Britain's Pippa Funnell picking up a well-deserved gold.

Equestrian events first entered the Games in 1912. The dressage, jumping and the three-day event were all included, but only for military riders – and then only commissioned officers in the dressage. The rule was strictly enforced, so much so that the Swedish gold medal winning team was disqualified in 1952 when it was discovered that one of the team was a non-commissioned officer. This led to the rules being changed for the next Olympics and justice was done when the same Swedish team won gold. In that year, civilians, including women, were at last allowed to compete. Immediately the sport benefited, as did Danish dressage rider, Lisa Hartel, who won silver, despite being paralysed below her knees as a result of polio, a truly astonishing achievement. Four years later she repeated the feat. Women have continued to do well in the sport, and in Seoul 1988, in a precursor of the 1999 European Eventing Championships result, three women picked up all three dressage medals.

WHAT TO **WATCH**

Dressage

The name is derived from the French verb dresser, which roughly means 'to train'. It can be likened to past events in figure skating when skaters had to complete compulsory figures on the ice, such as a figure of eight. Essentially, both horse and rider complete a number of movements at certain points of the arena. The rider dresses in top hat and tails and must show complete control over the horse. In each round, the rider performs a routine of movements, such as the pirouette, piaffe and passage, and a panel of judges mark them on their execution. The horse must demonstrate several changes of gait – the walk, the trot and the canter. The horse must be energetic yet calm, strong yet submissive, and precise in its movements. Dressage suits a rider with complete control and knowledge of the horse. The Germans are the world masters at dressage.

Jumping

While the dressage is often strictly for the purists, everyone, whether they have ridden a horse or not, can appreciate the jumping event. Competitors attempt a series of 15 to 20 jumps set out in an arena, usually very close together, and aim to finish the course without knocking any fences over. Some of the jumps are very intimidating and if the rider does not get the horse to jump at the right spot the horse will often balk at the fence and 'refuse'. If the horse jumps too early it will hit the obstacle with its hind legs, too late and it will hit the fence with its front ones. Jumps can be on their own or in quick succession, two or three at a time. They are not too solid so the horse won't get leg injuries, but this means even the slightest touch can bring part of a fence down and cost precious penalty points. Riders walk the course beforehand to plot the best point to take off at each obstacle and the quickest route.

Three-Day Event

The three-day event is in fact three different competitions, but all performed on the same horse. First comes the dressage, then comes the cross-country endurance test, the most dramatic part of the event. This is comprised of four parts; the first is a flat 4.4-kilometre road and track course, covered at a brisk trot or slow canter. It must be completed in a set time. The steeplechase follows, a 3105-

metre course featuring three brush fences that must be jumped three times and, once again, must be completed within a time limit. This is followed by another road and track section, longer than the first. The final part is the cross-country, over a 7.41-kilometre course. Horse and rider must clear up to 35 obstacles in a set time limit. Some of the jumps are more than a metre high and include perilous jumps over water, ditches and banks, though there is usually an easier but longer route round. The final event, should they make it, and many drop out before this stage, is the showjumping. Over a course of 10 to 12 obstacles, it is easier than the single showjumping event, but tough on a horse that has just completed the arduous cross-country section only the day before.

WHAT ARE THE **RULES?**

Dressage

The scoring for dressage is quite complicated. The five judges each score a move from zero to 10, 10 being the best score. The more difficult movements can earn double scores and judges also give a collective mark taking into account the aesthetic quality of the performance. In the Olympics, the first round is a Grand Prix test, which also doubles as the team competition. The riders follow a set routine of movements and the best 25 go forward to the next round, called the Grand Prix special, with the best 15 going into the final round, known as the Grand Prix freestyle. At this stage, riders perform a routine they have devised themselves that must last no longer than six minutes, accompanied by music they have chosen themselves. The team event is decided after the first round, based upon the three best individual scores from each team.

Jumping

A draw is made to determine the starting order. The object is to complete the course, regardless of style, with the fewest penalties for errors. The penalty points list is as follows:

- Four points for knocking down an obstacle or putting a foot in the water jump.

- Three points for refusing a jump, six points if it happens a second time, and elimination if it happens three times.

- Eight points if either horse or rider fall.

- Elimination if the horse refuses at a jump for longer than 60 seconds.

If a tie for the lead occurs then a jump-off takes place to decide the winner. The course is altered, and the obstacles moved or made higher. In the jump-off time enters the equation, with riders competing against the clock as well as the course. Should the number of penalties be the same then the rider with the fastest time wins.

Three-Day Event

Dressage – Riders must perform a set of 20 moves and are marked by judges for each move, taking into account how they controlled the horse and the obedience, pace and control of the animal. They are penalized for each error. All errors are then converted into penalty points to bring this section into line with the rest of the competition.

Cross-country – In the two road and track sections, one penalty point is awarded for every second a rider exceeds the time limit. In the steeplechase and on the cross-country course, one penalty point is awarded for every second over the time limit, 40 points are awarded if the horse refuses to jump an obstacle, a second refusal costs 80 points and a third refusal means disqualification. A fall costs 120 points and a second fall results in horse and rider being eliminated from the competition.

Jumping – Knocking down a gate costs 5 penalty points, refusal costs 10 penalty points.

The three-day event is an individual and a team event, held separately. The winner is the rider or the team with least penalty points at the end of the competition. A nation may enter four riders in a team but only the best three scores count. Riders may not, for the safety of the horse if nothing else, enter a horse in both the team and individual events. Should there be a tie at the end of the competition, the rider or the team with the best cross-country score is declared the winner.

WHO WILL **WIN?**

Britain's best medal chance is in the three-day event. Pippa Funnell, the European Champion, is a strong contender for the individual gold, as are team-mates Kristina Gifford, Polly Clark and Ian Stark. Together they will make a formidable challenge for the team gold. Funnell, Clark and Gifford were the only Europeans ranked in the world top 10 at the end of 1999. However, they will have to beat off a strong challenge from Australia – who have local knowledge and experience on the course – and New Zealand, for the team event, and New Zealanders Mark Todd and Andrew Nicholson for the individual gold. It promises to be a tense and exciting event.

Our best hope in the showjumping is John Whitaker, whose vast experience could help him to win a medal. The competition will be tough, with Brazilian Rodrigo Pessoa, the 1998 world showjumping champion installed as the favourite closely followed by Ludger Beerbaum of Germany. Beerbaum's compatriots dominate the dressage, though in recent years the Netherlands has been catching them up. The other nations are a long way behind, though Britain's Richard Davison will be hoping for a positive result.

DID YOU **KNOW?**

- At the 1956 Melbourne Olympics the equestrian events had to be held in Stockholm because of Australia's strict quarantine laws.

- In the 1932 Los Angeles Games, the three-day eventing course was so difficult that only two countries, the USA and the Netherlands, managed to finish. The bronze went unclaimed.

- In 1936 in Berlin, German Lieutenant Konrad von Wangenheim fell off his horse during the steeplechase and broke his collarbone, but remounted to finish the course. The next day he turned up with his arm in a sling but still competed in the showjumping. At the first fence he fell off and his horse fell on him. Both horse and rider got to their feet, completed the course and the German team won gold.

- In the 1932 dressage competition, Sweden's Bertil Sandstrom was relegated from second place when a judge detected a clicking noise he was using to guide his horse. Sandstrom was extremely upset because he claimed the noise was coming from his creaking saddle.

- The team three-day event actually takes four days – two days for dressage and a day each for the cross-country and showjumping.

BRITISH MEDAL COUNT

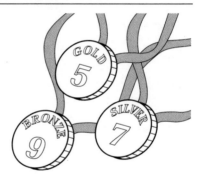

Fencing

16 – 24 September, Sydney Exhibition Centre

Fencing is one of only four sports to have featured in every modern Olympic Games since its creation in 1896. The Games' founder, Baron Pierre de Coubertin, invited a number of 'fencing masters' along to the first two events and the sport has been included ever since, adding some swash-buckling style to the proceedings. However, it is a sport that dates back long before 1896, to the days when the sword was the standard soldier's weapon.

Nowadays, things are somewhat different. Electronic equipment and hi-tech protective clothing are now vital parts of the sport, which requires lightning reflexes and a great deal of tactical nous. Fencers lunge, parry and riposte, probing for weaknesses in their opponent's armoury, hoping to score points and win the bout. Fencers need to be extremely light on their feet to dance away from attacks and need tremendous courage to attack, ignoring the clash of steel and their opponent's weapon inches from their face. One loss of concentration or balance can spell defeat.

In recent years, clear masks have been introduced into the event to allow spectators to see the combatants' faces;

previously they were hidden behind dense mesh masks. Coloured outfits have also been tested to bring the sport in line with the modern age. No quarter is spared in giving competitors the maximum amount of protection, though. Masks are made of perspex and stainless steel, and fencing jackets are lightweight yet immensely strong, all to avoid serious injury, which used to be a constant threat.

WHAT TO **WATCH**

There are three types of fencing weapons, after which the events are named – the foil, the sabre and the épée. Men, as individuals and in teams, compete in with all three, while women compete as individuals and in teams in the foil and épée only. The three events have different target areas:

The épée – The épée is the direct descendant of the duelling sword. The object in those duels was to draw blood and not deliver the killer blow and this is reflected in this event. Only hitting an opponent with the tip of the sword, with a pressure exceeding 750 grams, scores a point. A hit on the toe counts the same as one on the body. The sword possesses a guard to defend the hand and is the heaviest and stiffest of the three weapons.

The foil – This is the lightest of the three swords, which makes it difficult to handle. It originated as a training weapon for combat and the best scoring area is the torso. The tip of the foil must hit the opponent with a pressure exceeding 500 grams. Only the attacking fencer can score a point; if both fencers hit then the referee must decide who was doing the attacking. The defender can only score if the attack misses or is parried, and a counterattack succeeds.

The sabre – This weapon is derived from the cavalry sword, designed for slashing and thrusting. The target area is the entire body from the waist up, including the arms and mask, allowing fencers to use broadside cuts to register points. While the other events require quick, small movements, the sabre involves more obvious aggression and flamboyant swordplay. Often a fencer may attempt to run at his opponent, for example, but this is risky. The sabre, despite its dangerous sounding name, has a dull edge to minimize the risk of injury.

WHAT ARE THE **RULES?**

The bouts, consisting of three three-minute segments, take place on a 14×1.5-metre 'piste'. The fencers are connected to an electronic scoring system by use of wires and special clothing. A hit is worth one point, and a light shines on the scoreboard to indicate the fencer who was struck. The combatant with the most points wins. Forcing your opponent off the edge of the playing area can also score points. If the score is tied at the end of the bout, one minute of sudden-death overtime is played. To stop players being over-defensive during overtime, lots are drawn before the extra minute commences to determine who wins if nobody scores.

In team events, each team member fences against three members of the opposing team. Unless time runs out in a bout, the first one ends when a team reaches five points, the second at ten points and so on up to 45 points, or nine bouts. The winner is the first to reach 45 or has the most points at the end of nine bouts. When a bout stops, the fencers usually resume at the same spot on the piste prior to the stoppage, unless a fencer has conceded a one-metre penalty by putting both feet outside the boundaries of the piste. The offender then has to resume the bout one metre closer to the guilty party's end, giving them less room to manoeuvre.

Penalty points can be awarded against fencers if they jostle or turn their back on an opponent, leave the piste or use an unarmed hand to deflect a hit. Usually, a yellow card is issued first as a warning, followed by a red, which signals a penalty hit. More serious offences, like refusing to salute your opponent before a bout or cheating, can result in a black card and disqualification.

In Sydney, about 40 contestants will compete in the individual events. All are seeded, based upon their world ranking, and some receive byes (automatic entry into the next round) so that the first-round field has 32 competitors. The competition continues on the basis of a knockout tournament up to the semi-finals, which decide the medal places.

For the team event, eight to 12 teams take part. They are also seeded, but this time based on the results of the individual competition. If there are more than eight some receive first-round byes, so eight begin the tournament and a simple knockout tournament follows.

WHO WILL **WIN?**

Great Britain failed to perform well in the last World Championships and did not qualify for the individual or team events. Traditionally, the French have always possessed the most flamboyant and successful fencers, but the balance of power has shifted towards the Russians, who won four golds out of the six available for the men four years ago. Hungary and Italy are also strong. The glamour girl of the sport, Laura

Flessel-Colovic, who turned heads at Atlanta where she won gold in the individual and team épée competitions, will represent the French in the women's event.

DID YOU **KNOW?**

- Danger is always present in fencing. In the 1982 World Championships, Olympic foil gold medallist Vladimir Smirnov of the Soviet Union died when an opponent's sword pierced his mask.

- Fencers begin the bout with their masks off. The tradition dates back to duelling days when fighters had to identify themselves to show they had not sent another in their place.

- At the time of press it has not yet been decided, but electronic scoring equipment might be a thing of the past, starting in Sydney. A new radio-frequency system is being tested to see if it can be adapted in time for the Games, meaning the wires attached to fencers become obsolete.

- Bizarrely, the fencing competition of the 1924 Olympics actually led to a duel. The Italian team had a row over scoring with a Hungarian judge and matters came to a head at the Hungarian border after the Games. Two duels were fought, and wounds inflicted, before spectators fearing for the participants' lives stopped both.

Balestra: Short jump towards the opponent.

Beat: A sharp tap on an opponent's blade to initiate attack or the threat of attack.

Counter-parry: A defensive movement in which a fencer blocks a 'riposte' (attacking reply) from the opponent. There are many ways to parry a counterattack, including making a small circle with the tip of one's blade around the opponent's blade to deflect it.

Disengage: Break of contact between fencers' blades.

En garde: Fighting position taken up immediately before a bout begins.

Feint: A dummy attack intended to open up an opponent to a genuine attack.

Fleche: A short run towards the opponent.

Lunge: Most common attack, in which the fencer closes the distance by moving their front leg forward while the back leg remains stationary and straight.

Parry: Defensive action in which a fencer blocks his or her opponent's thrust.

Piste: French term (meaning 'track') for the long, narrow strip on which the competition takes place.

Recover: Return to the en garde position after a lunge.

Remise: Attacking again immediately after an opponent's parry of an initial attack.

Right-of-way: The right-of-way rule is used in the foil and sabre events, and was established to eliminate apparently simultaneous attacks by two fencers; épée does not use this rule.

Riposte: Defender's counterattack after parrying an attack.

Thrust: The quick extension of the sword blade without foot movement.

BRITISH MEDAL COUNT

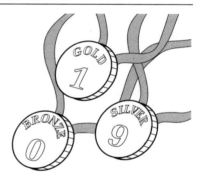

GOLD 1

BRONZE 0

SILVER 9

Football

Women's Final: 28 September, Olympic Stadium
Men's Final: 30 September, Olympic Stadium

Fittingly, the most popular sport in the world will be the first event at the Olympics, with the first round of matches actually being played before the opening ceremony. It is also the only sport in the Games that is not based in Sydney alone. Matches will be played across Australia, in Adelaide, Brisbane, Canberra, Melbourne, as well as Sydney, giving Australian fans their first chance of watching an international tournament. The crowds for the event promise to be huge, not least for the women's competition. This might be to do with the injection of glamour into the game by the Australian women's football team (originally known as the 'Matildas') who caused controversy in Australia by recently appearing nude in a calendar.

Football, together with water polo, was one of the first team sports to be introduced into the Olympics, way back in 1900, and was won by England, who also picked up the gold in 1908 and 1912 – the last time they have done so. This is because in recent years teams from Europe have been selected for the Olympics by virtue of their performances in the European under-21 Championships and England have failed to qualify. Four places are up for grabs this time, so the winner, runners-up and semi-final losers in this summer's European Under-21 Championships will make it through to Sydney. The gold medal is usually won by a European team apart from in 1924 and 1928 when Uruguay won, and in Atlanta four years ago when the Nigerians proved that African football had improved considerably and was becoming a major world force.

WHAT TO **WATCH**

Sixteen teams contest the men's competition, eight contest the women's. For the men, like Euro 2000, the teams are divided into four pools for a round-robin preliminary tournament, with the top two from each going through to the quarter-finals. From that point on, the tournament is a straight knockout competition culminating in the final which will be held at the Olympic Stadium in Sydney on 30 September.

The women's tournament is similar to the men's, except that the top two teams from each group advance straight to the semi-finals. The women's final will be held at the Sydney Football Stadium on 28 September. It is anticipated that the women's tournament will attract huge crowds like it did in Atlanta four years ago, the first time the women's game appeared in the Olympics. Then, 76,000 fans turned up to watch the USA take the gold medal, a world record attendance for the women's game.

WHAT ARE THE **RULES?**

In the modern day and age, those people who have managed to avoid watching football are a rare breed. The rules for the Olympic competition are exactly the same as for any other major international football competitions but with one important difference. All players must be under 23 years old, apart from three exceptions who can be any age. The rule was pressed for by FIFA (football's world governing body) to ensure that the World Cup remained the most prestigious tournament of them all. The only restriction for the women's tournament is that players must be over 16 years of age.

WHO WILL **WIN?**

At the time of writing, a number of the qualifiers for the men's tournament had not yet been decided. England were poised for a good performance at the finals of the European Under-21 Football Championships, with every chance of picking up one of the four spots in Sydney. It is dependent, however, on how many of their star players were selected for the senior championship tournament. If the likes of West Ham's Frank Lampard, teenage sensation Joe Cole and Leicester's Emille Heskey are not available for the under-21s then England may struggle against the likes of Spain, the World Youth Champions, and Germany.

If England qualify it will be interesting to see who they pick as their three over-23 players, as the Premiership season will be underway and few managers will want to see their young stars swelter in the Sydney heat with a long campaign in England ahead.

The Central and South American sides will also fancy their chances. Brazil, as we all know, possess some fantastic talent and constantly produce young players of great flair. Unbelievably, given their illustrious past, they have never won Olympic gold. They take international competition seriously and will do everything they can to win this one. They will almost certainly be the side to beat. Argentina, runners-up in Atlanta, will be hoping to go one better than last time while Nigeria will hope their current crop of young players prove as thrilling and successful as the squad that won gold in Atlanta, providing great entertainment en route. Australia, Japan, South Korea and Kuwait are the outsiders, though Leeds United's Australian forward Harry Kewell and Birmingham City winger Stan Lazaridis will be attempting to make sure that their side is not humiliated.

The Australians have a far better chance in the women's competition, though the USA are the favourites. They won the Women's World Cup last year in style and look likely to dominate in Sydney, possessing the women's answer to Ronaldo in the shape of Mia Hamm. China and Norway, who like the men's team play a very direct style of football, will be hoping to challenge them.

DID YOU **KNOW?**

- The Olympic Football Tournament gave birth to the World Cup. It used to be the only international competition until FIFA was born in 1930 and established its own world competition.

- The record for the number of goals scored in one game by one person in the Olympics is 10, achieved in 1908 by

Denmark's Sophus Nielsen, against France, and equalled by Gottfried Fuchs of Germany, against Russia, four years later.

- People who believe the Olympic tournament means nothing to European football fans are wrong. More than 100,000 people turned up at the Nou Camp stadium in Barcelona in 1992 to watch Spain win gold by beating Italy 1–0.

- In 1936 at the Berlin Olympics, Peru withdrew its entire Olympic team from the Games after a bizarre incident during the nation's football match against Austria. With the match level at 2–2, some Peruvian fans invaded the pitch and attacked an Austrian player. In the confusion that followed, Peru scored twice to lead 4–2 and won the game. Austria protested, their appeal was upheld and a rematch ordered – behind closed doors. Peru chose not to turn up, were thrown out of the competition and in response withdrew their whole Olympic contingent.

BRITISH MEDAL COUNT

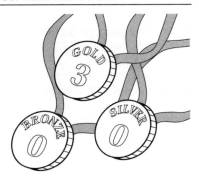

GOLD 3

BRONZE 0

SILVER 0

Gymnastics

Artistic Gymnastics: 14 – 26 September, Sydney SuperDome
Rhythmic Gymnastics: 26 September – 1 October, Pavilion 2
Trampoline: 22 – 23 September, Sydney SuperDome

The gymnastic event in Sydney has got bigger with the introduction of the trampoline event for the first time in Olympic history. Not that the gymnastic event ever needed more spicing up, as it is one of the most popular and eagerly-awaited events of the Games. It has a glittering history filled with remarkable achievements, the most famous being at the 1976 Olympics in Montreal where Romanian Nadia Comeneci took the sport by storm. She was the first gymnast in history to record a 10 (the perfect score) – and then went on to achieve the feat six more times on her way to the gold medal. That stunning success cemented the excitement surrounding the sport created four years earlier by the Soviet Union's Olga Korbut, who completed a back flip on the beam (see below), something no one had ever seen before. Gymnastics' past is nothing if not illustrious.

However, the sport has a history that goes back much further than the days of Korbut and Comeneci. It was part of the ancient Games, where the all male performers competed naked. In fact, it is from those early days that the sport derived its name, since 'gymnos' is the Greek word for naked.

In the Roman era such abandon was frowned upon and the sport was banned for being immoral. It was not until the sixteenth century that it returned (clothed), as a form of street entertainment, and in the early 1800s the precursor of the sport we know today emerged, named artistic gymnastics, which still remains the sport's full title. Competitions flourished across Europe in the late nineteenth century and when the modern Olympics began in 1896 it was made an Olympic sport once more. The five events were the horizontal bar, pommel horse, rings, vault and parallel bars (see below), all still used today by the men. Alongside those well-known events were less conventional gymnastic disciplines, such as rope climbing and swinging clubs.

In 1924, the Olympic gymnastic programme became settled, with men competing as individuals and teams on set pieces of apparatus, and four years later, a women's event was introduced.

Rhythmic gymnastics appeared at the 1984 Olympics, 22 years after the gymnastics' governing board recognized it as an official sport. It has made a graceful and balletic contribution to the Games ever since. And now the trampoline has been added, a sport that allegedly derived from the Eskimo practice of bouncing on walrus skins. The trampoline first made its name in the circus, but grew as a sport over the last century. Its first World Championships were held in London in 1958 and now it is part of one of the great Olympic competitions.

ARTISTIC GYMNASTICS

The standard of gymnastics has risen enormously over the years, so that the margin for error is very small; dropping half a point can lead to a competitor falling behind. The men compete on six items of 'apparatus', the women compete on four.

These are:

MEN

Floor

The floor is 12 metres square. Judges look out for spectacular acrobatics and 'tumbling', including somersaults, twists, pikes and tucks. Unlike the women, the men do not perform their routine to music. They simply run, jump and leap in the 60 to 70 seconds they are allowed to complete their routine. At least one show of strength must be included, such as balancing on the floor with only one arm. A fall, slip or loss of balance can cost precious points.

Vault

The vault is one of the more high-octane gymnastic events. This piece of apparatus involves a long run up to a springboard from which the gymnast leaps, using his hands to push off the vault and then complete a somersault in the air before trying to execute a perfect landing. Judges look for the amount of height gained and distance travelled through the air. Again, a slip on landing can be costly.

Rings

The rings hang by cables 2.55 metres above the floor. A good rings routine requires massive amounts of strength. Gymnasts will attempt to combine a series of moves, including swinging up to a handstand, suspending themselves stock still in a crucifix position and a range of spectacular dismounts. Any sign of the rings wobbling, or competitors' arms shaking, costs points.

Parallel Bars

This apparatus, 1.82 metres off the floor, tests the dexterity and agility of the gymnast. They move around the bars at such high speed that the whole routine can be a blur. Look out for moves that involve releasing the grip on the bars completely before grabbing hold once more. Different competitors will find different ways to launch themselves on and off the bars.

Horizontal Bar (or High Bar)

The men swing around the 2.55m high bar at high speed, alternating direction, leaping high into the air and then grabbing the bar on their descent. This is one of the most spectacular gymnastic routines. The grand finale comes with the dismount, which has become increasingly elaborate and difficult to perform perfectly.

Pommel Horse

Suspending their whole weight with their hands, the competitors swing their legs in circular and scissors-like movements over the back of the horse, changing their grip every second. Much of the routine is spent on one hand as the other searches for a platform to launch the next move. The hands are the only part of the body that are allowed to touch the horse.

WOMEN

Vault

This is basically the same as the men's vault, except that the vaulting horse is turned sideways rather than lengthways.

Uneven Bars (or Isometric Bars)

One bar is situated 2.5 metres off the floor, the other 1.65 metres, parallel to each other. The gymnasts alternate between the two, letting go of one bar and catching the other as they pass. No more than four consecutive moves can be done on one bar. Often the gymnasts will use the lower bar to halt their swing, wrapping their bodies around it to lever themselves in the opposite direction. Watch for the spectacular dismounts, usually after momentum has been built up by some prolonged high-speed swinging.

Beam

A true test of balance, the beam is just 10 centimetres wide, which would make it difficult for most of us to walk across, never mind perform a series of jumps, somersaults and turns. This can often be the apparatus that determines success or failure, because falling off can cause a number of points to be lost. The routine lasts between 70 and 90 seconds, and the judges expect to see a number of high-risk moves.

Floor

Unlike the men, the women perform to music, and a good choice can have the crowds clapping and cheering every move. In addition to the tumbling, the women must show grace in their movements and look as if they are enjoying what they are doing which can lead to some very theatrical performances.

RHYTHMIC GYMNASTICS

Rhythmic gymnastics is a women-only event and has accurately been described as a form of ballet on a mat. Rhythmic gymnasts perform with, rather than on, a piece of apparatus. All the events take place on a 13-metre-square floor. Gymnasts receive individual scores for each piece of apparatus, but the medals are awarded to whoever possesses the highest total score after all pieces of apparatus have been used. The four pieces of apparatus used are the rope, hoop, ball and ribbon. In addition, during the team event, clubs can be used.

TRAMPOLINING

For starters, the ceiling of the building the trampoline is used in must be eight metres high to avoid competitors banging their heads on it. Each routine must display 10 recognized skills, which include:

- One landing on either the front or the back of the body.

- A single or a double somersault, or something in between containing at least a 540-degree twist.

- A forwards or a backwards somersault.

- A somersault that includes at least a full twist.

In the trampoline event, like diving, style is just as important as the substance of the routine. Artistry and grace play as big a part as mastering the technicalities.

ARTISTIC GYMNASTICS

There are three types of competition for both men and women – team, all-round individual and separate events for each piece of apparatus. In the team competition, a gymnast is allowed just one attempt at each piece of apparatus, except for the women's vault where two attempts are allowed and the score averaged out. Two panels of judges rate all performances in all events. One panel contains two 'difficulty' judges who assess how hard a routine is and award it a rating out of 10, with 10 being the most difficult and the most common rating in the Olympics. The other panel contains six judges who mark each performance on its technical execution. They deduct points from the score determined by the difficulty judges if they spot any errors or minor flaws in a routine. Minor errors cost 0.10 of a point, 0.20 to 0.30 for medium errors and 0.40 for large errors. The worst error of all, falling, costs 0.50 points. The highest and lowest scores are discarded and a final score achieved by taking an average of the other four scores.

In the team and all-round individual competitions, the scores for each piece of apparatus are added together to give a total score. The best score for each piece of apparatus is ten, so with men competing on six pieces the maximum score is 60, while it is 40 for the women because they only compete on four pieces of apparatus. In the team event, the top four scores count, out of a team of six, making 40 the maximum team score for each apparatus.

Following a qualification round, the top six teams advance to the final, where the highest score wins. Each team has six gymnasts but only five can perform on each piece of apparatus. For the individual finals, the top eight from the qualification round on each piece of apparatus go through to contest the medals on that piece of apparatus. For example, during the qualification round, the best eight scorers on the rings will compete in the final for medals. For the all-round individual events the top 36 men and 36 women in the qualification round, based on their combined scores for each piece of apparatus, advance to the finals. They compete on each piece of apparatus and the person with the highest combined scores wins the medal.

RHYTHMIC GYMNASTICS

Three panels of judges monitor the rhythmic gymnastics. One set, the technical judges, marks the difficulty of a routine, one evaluates the artistic merit, while the other set observes the execution of the routine. Artistic marks are awarded for originality, choreography, the choice of apparatus, and the musical accompaniment. The execution judges look for how well movements were conducted, how the apparatus was used and the degree of perfection involved.

The technical and the artistic judges mark each routine out of five, while the execution judges mark it out of 10. The points are added together to produce a total, which is then halved to produce a score out of 10.

Scoring differs for the team event, with more emphasis put on the artistic side of a routine. The technical judges mark out of four, the artistic judges out of six and the execution judges still mark out of 10. The final score is not halved so it remains a score out of 20.

Gymnasts lose points for errors. For 'slight uncertainties or lack of precision' 0.05 is deducted, 0.10 is taken away for small faults, 0.20 for medium mistakes and 0.30 for major errors. Points can also be lost in the event of a gymnast stepping beyond the boundaries of the floor area or losing control of the apparatus.

The individual event comprises 24 gymnasts, while the team event consists of 10 teams of six members. The highest score in each event wins the gold.

TRAMPOLINING

Seven judges score a trampoline routine. Five of them rate how well the different moves were performed during the routine, while two rate their degree of difficulty. Points are awarded for the performances, and then adjusted according to the degree of difficulty involved. Like the other events, the five judges monitoring the performance deduct points from 10 for any faults or imperfections they detect. Some errors mean an automatic deduction, such as touching the trampoline with the hands which results in 0.4 points being lost, or falling on a safety platform (placed to prevent competitors from bouncing off the trampoline and onto the floor), which costs 0.8 points.

The degree of difficulty is calculated by the number of somersaults and twists completed in a routine. A full somersault is worth 0.4 points, a three-quarter somersault is worth 0.3. A full twist scores 0.2, a half twist 0.1. If the two moves are combined then the difficulty value increases. The two judges come up with a difficulty rating, which usually ranges between 11 and 15. The execution judges' lowest and highest marks are discarded, and the remaining three added together, and then added to the difficulty rating. A perfect score would be 45.

Only individuals, rather than teams, will compete in Sydney. Both the men's and women's events will feature 12 competitors who will perform a compulsory routine to demonstrate set skills, and an optional routine in which the gymnast can choose some of the moves they wish to perform. The highest points scorer wins.

WHO WILL **WIN?**

Great Britain received a huge boost last year when the women's team finished in eleventh place in the World Championships in China, earning a place for the team at the Olympics for the first time. The team is made up of Lisa Mason, who finished twenty-sixth in the all-round event in China, British all-round champion Annika Reeder, Sharna Murrey, Natalie Lucitt, Rochelle Douglas and Holly Murdock. Although the team finished ahead of both Germany and Belarus a medal in Sydney would be expecting too much. Russia and China are the favourites to take the team crown, though the Ukraine will be pressing hard. Individually, look out for Anna Kovalyova of Russia and China's Ling Jie and Liu Xuan in the all-round competition, though Ukraine's reigning gold medal holder Liliya Podkopayeva will not relinquish her crown lightly.

Unfortunately, Britain's men failed to emulate the women and the team did not qualify. Their nineteenth position in China means that only one gymnast from Britain will attend Games. Romantics will hope it is Craig Heap, who fell during the 1996 Olympic trials and failed to make the Games, nearly forcing him to quit the sport. Now he is back and in with a great chance of representing his country. Once again, Russia

135

and China should dominate, though the Ukraine, Belarus, USA and France could all do well.

Great Britain's young rhythmic gymnastic teams failed to qualify for Sydney, but the World Championships were their first taste of major international competition and they will benefit from the experience. Favourite for the individual title is Alina Kabaeva of Russia, the country also tipped to win the team competition. Their biggest threat comes from Belarus.

Lee Brearley and Jaime Moore will be our representatives in the men and women's trampoline. Both qualified on the basis of good placings in the World Trampolining Championships, held in South Africa last year. Brearley will need to excel to win a medal. Reigning world champion Alexandre Moskalenko of Russia is the one to beat. Moore has an outside chance of a medal, but she'll have to improve on her ninth place in the World Championships, where another Russian, Irina Karavaera, took the gold.

DID YOU **KNOW?**

- In 1976 at Montreal, Japanese gymnast Shun Fujimoto broke his kneecap during the floor routine. Not wanting to let his team down, he told no one and, hiding his pain, scored 9.5 on the pommel horse and then moved onto the rings where he attempted a triple somersault dismount. He only buckled slightly on landing and earned 9.7 from the judges, his best score ever. It mattered too, as Japan went on to win the gold by only 0.40 points. Asked a few years later if he would do it again, he succinctly replied, 'No'.

- In 1988, Russian Dmitri Bilozerchev remarkably won two gold medals, despite having to recover from a car accident a few years earlier that broke his leg in 40 places.

- In 1904 in St Louis, American George Eyser won two gold medals in the parallel bars and the vault. The catch? He had a wooden leg.

JARGON BUSTER – RHYTHMIC GYMNASTICS

Amplitude: The height, flight, distance or body angles displayed by a gymnast performing a skill. In general, the bigger or higher, the better.

Composition: The structure of a routine; that is, how each movement or skill is fitted together to create a complete exercise.

Execution: Form, style and the technique displayed during the performance of a routine.

Mills: Small figure-eight circles performed with the clubs.

Roll: An acrobatic move in which the body is rolled forwards, backwards or sideways, or the rolling of an apparatus such as a ball or hoop on the body or on the floor.

Rotation: Any turning, spinning or circling movement of a piece of apparatus.

Snakes: A zig-zag pattern formed by the ribbon as it moves through the air. This can be done at any angle.

Spirals: A coil pattern using the ribbon to make up of a series of small circles.

Taps: A sound produced by hitting the clubs together or on the floor.

JARGON BUSTER – TRAMPOLINE

Ballout: Any forward rotating skill which starts after the gymnast's back makes contact with the trampoline.

Barani: A half-twisting single front somersault.

Cody: Any somersaulting skill that starts after the stomach makes contact with the trampoline.

Fliffis: A half-twisting double front somersault.

Full: A full-twisting single back somersault.

Miller: A triple-twisting double back somersault.

Miller Plus: A quadruple-twisting double back somersault.

Randy: A 2½-twisting single front somersault.

Routine: A combination of movements displaying a full range of skills.

Rudy: A 1½-twisting single front somersault.

Triffis: A half-twisting triple front somersault.

BRITISH MEDAL COUNT

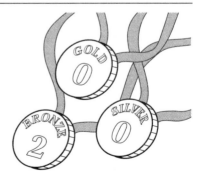

138

Handball

16 September – 1 October, Pavilion 2

Handball can be seen as a hybrid of three different sports: basketball, football and hockey. As a sport, it has been completely dominated by European nations, unsurprising since it was invented to keep Dutch football players fit when the soccer season was over. It certainly works – it is fast and physical, with quick passing, and shooting speeds of up to 70mph.

Despite being relatively unknown in the UK, the game has a great global appeal. It is played in about 160 countries by around eight million people, though, like football, it has failed to catch on in America.

Handball is a thoroughly modern game. The first international match was played in 1925, and just 11 years later it was part of the Olympic Games in Berlin.

In those days, the game was 11-a-side and mainly played outdoors on football pitches. A smaller version featuring seven players per side, played on an indoor court, soon gained popularity and displaced the original format, which died out in 1966.

The game had disappeared off the Olympic schedule, too, but was reinstated for men in 1972, and four years later, a women's competition was added.

The game has many similarities to football in that the key to success lies in precise, quick passing. The players work together to move the ball up the court towards the opposition goal, and do so much quicker than their soccer or basketball counterparts. This leads to a large amount of shots being taken and the total number of goals scored in a match can often reach 40. Like basketball, players rely on feints, body swerves, and huge leaps in the air to pass, control the ball and shoot. Unlike basketball, however, physical contact is allowed and legal body-checks can sometimes see players crashing to the ground without any foul being committed.

The seven players all have positions. Firstly, there is a goalkeeper who has the unenviable task of keeping out the very powerful shots being thrown at him. Three players play at the back, in the left, middle and right positions. Their job is to get the ball up the court to break down the opposition's defence. The left and right backs are usually the game's highest scorers, advancing forward while the centre back sweeps up behind them, prompting attacks and covering counterattacks. The two wingers are the quickest players and stick to the sides of the court to deliver leaping cross-court passes. The final player is called a circle runner, who has a free role around the court, and in defence will usually man-mark the opposition's best player or highest scorer and attempt to disrupt the opposition's game plan.

The most spectacular part of handball is probably the penalty throw, similar in many respects to a penalty kick in football. This is a head-to-head confrontation between shooter and 'keeper from the seven-metre line and is awarded when a serious foul has been committed. The player must hurl the ball into the net, which is three metres wide and two metres high, while the goalkeeper must try to keep out the blurred object flashing towards him.

WHAT ARE THE **RULES?**

A handball match consists of two 30-minute halves. The players aim to get the ball into the opposition's goal without entering the goal area, which is D-shaped and six metres from the goal itself. Players can use any part of the body to move the ball, apart from their lower legs and feet. The ball can be taken forward by running with it, though players are limited to three steps before they must pass, dribble or shoot. If a player stops dribbling they have three seconds to pass or shoot. If a player jumps, they must pass or shoot before landing.

For minor offences, such as overstepping, a free throw is awarded from the place the infringement occurred. At a free throw, opposition players must retreat three metres. If the infringement takes place within the free throw area, which is nine metres from the goal, the attacking players must retreat to the edge of the free throw area before taking the throw to allow the opposition to move back the mandatory three metres without stepping into their own goal area. A penalty throw is awarded when more serious offences, such as illegal interference when a player is shooting, take place. If the ball goes out of bounds, a throw-in is awarded against the team to last touch the ball. If the ball goes over the goal-line and an attacking player was the last to touch it, it goes to the 'keeper. If a defensive player was the last to touch the ball, a corner throw is awarded to the opposition.

Other rules include:

- Goalkeepers can use any part of their body, including the feet, to stop the ball. They can also take as many steps as they want to before releasing the ball from their goal area.

- Players cannot throw the ball out of play deliberately.

- Players given yellow cards for fouls are suspended from play for two minutes. If they repeatedly offend they are given a red card and sent off. However, unlike football, after two minutes the expelled player can be replaced by a substitute. For extremely serious offences, like fighting, a player can be excluded, the highest form of punishment, and no replacement is allowed.

- Teams possess five substitutes which can be used at any time and as often as the coach wishes.

- Each team is granted a one-minute timeout per half.

In Sydney, the 12 men's teams, and 10 women's, will be divided into two pools. The teams play each other once, and the top four teams from each pool advance into the quarter-finals. The competition is then a straight knockout.

WHO WILL **WIN?**

In the men's competition, the winner will almost certainly come from Europe. In some countries, the players are treated as heroes in the same way as their wealthier football compatriots. Sweden are the current world champions and look a good bet to emulate that feat in Sydney, though they will come up against stiff opposition from Russia, Yugoslavia and Belarus while Egypt and Japan will probably be the best of the non-European sides.

Reigning Olympic and world champions Denmark dominate the women's game, although they will be hoping to avoid their Scandinavian neighbours, Norway, en route to the final. South Korea are the one non-European side to have won Olympic gold and will be hoping to do well again, while Hungary will also be chasing a medal.

DID YOU **KNOW?**

- In Spain, handball players are treated like royalty. In fact, one of them is. Veteran Onaki Urgangarin is otherwise known as the Duke of Palma de Mallorca.

- The only player allowed to dive for the ball is the goalkeeper. All other players must always keep on their feet, unless jumping.

- A player can body-check an opponent even if the opponent does not have the ball. However, a player may not use their arms or legs to impede other players or steal the ball from their hands.

Hockey

16 – 30 September, State Hockey Centre

It was one of the most memorable Olympic moments that Great Britain has experienced in recent times. In 1988, in Seoul, Great Britain's men were leading against the Germans, the strong favourites, by 1–0 in the final. As the second, winning goal was fired into the net in the second half, BBC commentator Barry Davies lost his usual sense of neutrality. 'Where, oh where were the Germans?' he asked, before adding after a short pause, 'And frankly, who cares?' He fully captured the euphoria of England's unlikely gold medal achievement, and the joy of a national side finally beating the Germans in an important international sporting event.

Hockey was first introduced into the Olympics in London in 1908 and won by Great Britain, who also took the title in 1988. The sport was an irregular addition to the schedules until 1928 when it became a permanent fixture, much to the delight of India, who between 1928 and 1956 won six consecutive gold medals. By 1960, they had played 30 Olympic matches and won them all, but were stunned in the final by arch-rivals Pakistan, who took the top prize, winning 1–0. While people rejoiced on the streets of Pakistan, the population of India went into mass mourning, treating the defeat as a national tragedy. However, it was not until 1972, for the first time in 52 years, that a country other than India and Pakistan won the gold medal; West Germany took the prize in Munich. Eight years later, women's hockey was added to the Olympic programme and the sport became one of the most popular Olympic events.

Hockey evolved in its modern form in Britain during the nineteenth century and became a popular sport at English public schools. It was then taken around the world by the British army, hence its popularity in India and Pakistan. Not for the first time, a game the British successfully exported became a sport in which they ended up being soundly beaten. In fact, the origins of the sport may go back much further than this. Apparently, archaeologists have found sketches in Egypt of people playing a version of the game some 4000 years ago. This makes hockey the oldest ball-and-stick game in the world. It is also one of the most fiercely competitive. Shinguards and mouthguards are both essential pieces of equipment for avoiding injury from swinging sticks and the hard ball, while goalkeepers' bodies are trussed up in huge pads, body protectors, gloves and a mask to protect them from shots that can reach speeds of 90mph.

WHAT TO **WATCH**

Hockey bears little resemblance to ice hockey, other than in the shape of the sticks. The outdoor game, which Americans refer to as field hockey, is 11-a-side, played over two 35-minute halves, and has the objective of getting the ball into the opponents' goal. Like football, most games are generally low-scoring affairs and many goals come from set pieces, such as corners or penalties. Passing is the key to success from the defensive backs, through the midfield to the forwards, who usually score all the goals and grab all the glory.

WHAT ARE THE **RULES?**

Only the 'keeper is allowed to use his hands; all other players must only make contact with the ball using their sticks. Touching the ball with any other part of the body yields a foul. Players must only use the flat front face of the stick; it is illegal to use the rounded back side. During the normal run of play, goals can only be scored from within the scoring circle, which is a semi-circle, 16 yards in front of goal. The game does have some quirks the casual observer must know in order to fully understand what is going on. These are:

1. Long corners and penalty corners
If a defender hits the ball unintentionally over their own back-line then a long corner is awarded to the attacking team. The ball is placed on a spot about five metres (the exact distance depends on the size of the pitch) in from the corner flag on the back-line and the attacking side hits it back into play and attempts to score.

However, if the defender hits the ball intentionally over the back-line, then a penalty corner is awarded to the attacking side. The ball is placed on the back-line, about nine metres from the nearest goalpost, and the attacking side is given a free hit. The ball is usually struck to the edge of the goal circle, where one player will set up the shot for another to try and score. This provides some of the game's most spectacular moments. The defence can have five players, including the goalie, behind the back-line who rush out to block the shot. Getting in the way of the ball can result in some very bad injuries, though a shot from a penalty corner must not hit the net higher than the backboard in the goal, which is 18 inches above the ground.

2. Penalties

Penalties are awarded if a defending player commits an intentional offence within the goal circle that prevents a goal being scored, or an unintentional offence that stops an attacker from scoring a goal. The ball is placed on a spot seven yards from the goal and the attacker shoots with only the goalkeeper to beat.

3. Dangerous Play

A lot of pain can be inflicted with a hockey stick, so to minimize injuries, dangerous play is outlawed. Players cannot lift any part of their sticks above head height even when playing the ball or wield them in a dangerous manner. The ball cannot generally be hit up in the air unless a player is shooting, though the game's two referees can use their discretion as to what constitutes a dangerous height. Among other decision, they also rule on obstruction, when a player uses his or her body or stick to impede an opponent.

Other rules include:

- For dangerous play, misconduct or intentional fouls, players can be awarded a green card, which constitutes a warning, a yellow card which results in a five-minute suspension, or a red card, which results in the player being sent-off for the rest of the game.

- A substituted player can re-enter the game at any time.

In Sydney, the tournament will include 12 men's teams and 10 women's teams, split into two pools. For the men, each team plays the other teams in its pool once, with the top two sides advancing to the semi-finals. The semi-final winners contest the gold and silver medals, while the losers play-off for the bronze. The others play a classification round to determine the placings between 5th and 12th. The top three teams from each of the two women's pools advance into another pool of six. These teams play each other once with the top two sides playing for the gold, while the teams ranked third and fourth play-off for bronze.

WHO WILL **WIN?**

Although both Great Britain's men's and women's teams should qualify for Sydney, both teams face a tough battle to win a medal. In the women's tournament, Australia are the dominant force and home advantage may make them unstoppable. They have been the best team for almost a decade, winning golds in 1988 and 1996, as well as winning the last two World Cups. Germany, South Korea and the Netherlands, as well as Great Britain, may well be battling it out for silver and bronze.

The men's competition is more open, though the Australians will also be heavily favoured after winning the 1999 Champions Trophy. The reigning Olympic champions are the Netherlands, who will be very strong, as will Spain and Germany. Britain defeated Germany last year but will have to play very well to win a medal in Sydney.

DID YOU **KNOW?**

- The name hockey is derived from the French 'hoquet', an old word for a shepherd's crook.

- During India's remarkable run of success between 1928 and 1956, no fewer than five players named Balbir Singh played in the team. The first Balbir Singh scored five goals in the 6–1 thrashing of the Netherlands in 1928.

- The synthetic playing surface used hockey is supposed to be wet. Water is sprinkled onto it before the game and at half-time. If the field is not watered, friction stops the small ball moving across the pitch easily.

BRITISH MEDAL COUNT

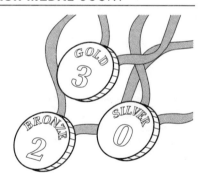

Judo

16 – 22 September, Sydney Exhibition Centre

As the translation of the word suggests – it is Japanese for 'the gentle way' – judo is not about dealing knockout blows to an opponent. However, the rules still allow contestants to gain a submission by breaking an opponent's arm or by choking them, so perhaps 'gentle' is not quite the right word.

Judo was started in the 1880s by Jigoro Kano. A young man who had studied the ancient martial art of ju-jitsu, he opened a school of his own teaching a new art named judo, developed from his expertise and knowledge of ju-jitsu. It became a government approved sport when 15 of Kano's students travelled across Japan demonstrating it. At the end of a demonstration, the lecturer would fight a member of the local training school, using his judo skills. In 1886, a match was held to see which form of ju-jitsu should be taught at public, police and military schools. Kano's students defeated all-comers and the sport was officially born.

In Britain, the sport gained a foothold at the beginning of the last century, after a number of Japanese 'showmen' toured the country demonstrating the sport. Many of the showmen stayed, wrote books on the sport and taught it.

From these beginnings the sport has grown widely, so that even the British Conservative Party leader, William Hague, uses it to keep fit, fighting his colleague and former gold medal-winning runner-turned-politician, Sebastian Coe.

Judo spread across the world in the same way as in Britain. It became an Olympic sport at the 1964 Tokyo Games when the host nation was allowed to add one new sport to the schedule. Japan won three of four gold medals available. The only one Japan didn't win was taken by a giant Dutchman, Antonius Geesink. It was he, after using his massive frame to win the 1961 World Championships, who encouraged the introduction of weight divisions to make the sport fairer.

In 1992, the women's judo competition started and women now compete in as many weight classes as the men, seven in total. 400 athletes will contest the gold medal in Sydney, showing the sport's huge popularity.

WHAT TO **WATCH**

Contests last five minutes for men, four minutes for women. The two contestants, known as judoka, attempt to score a point by throwing their opponent, or applying a hold that immobilizes them for 25 seconds. The first contestant to score a point wins the bout. If no one scores a point then the athlete who has won half a point is the winner (see below), and if no one scores any points at all, the bout is decided on how many credits the contestants have scored with the judges.

There are seven weight classes for both men and women, which are as follows:

Extra lightweight – under 60kg for men, under 48kg for women

Half lightweight – under 66kg for men, under 52kg for women

Lightweight – under 73kg for men, under 57kg for women

Half middleweight – under 81kg for men, under 63kg for women

Middleweight – under 90kg for men, under 70kg for women

Half heavyweight – under 100kg for men, under 78kg for women

Heavyweight – more than 100kg for men, more than 78kg for women

All competitors in each division are split into two pools and then fight a series of knockout bouts. The two finalists compete for gold and silver. All judokas who lose to the finalists compete in a repechage (French for 'second chance') within their own pools. The winner of each pool faces the runner-up in the opposing pool to decide who takes the two bronze medals on offer.

WHAT ARE THE **RULES?**

A victory, achieved by scoring one point, is called an ippon. To score an ippon with a throw, the opponent must be thrown mainly onto their back with control, force and speed. If one of these four criteria is missing then a half-point is awarded, known as a waza-ari. A half-point can also be scored for a hold that lasts more than 20, but less than 25, seconds.

Contestants can also score using a yuko or a koka. A yuko is earned with a throw in which two of the above criteria are missing or by a hold that lasts between 15 and 19 seconds. A koka is awarded if three of the criteria for a throw are not met, or with a hold that lasts between 10 and 14 seconds. If a bout is drawn, then the number of yuko and koka are counted up. Yuko is counted first, but if this score is the same, then koka are counted. If there is still a tie, the judges vote for a winner by taking into account the aggression shown by each combatant and the effectiveness of their combat. Then either a white or blue flag is held up signalling the colour of person who won the bout, the contestants having been assigned either blue or white at the start.

Penalties play a major part in judo, and contestants are punished in different ways, ranging from awarding an opponent a koka for small offences, to an ippon for the most serious, though the referee must confer with the judges before imposing such a penalty. Penalties can be imposed for not showing enough aggression, dangerous play, or pushing a contestant off the 46-foot-square playing mat. However, a contestant can throw an opponent out of the playing area as long as the thrower stays within it.

Other rules include:

- Judoka must bow to each other before and after a bout.

- A judoka locked in a hold submits by tapping twice on the mat with either hand or foot.

- If a bout is stopped due to an injury to a judoka, and the opponent is clearly to blame for it, then the latter loses the bout.

WHO WILL **WIN?**

Great Britain has a solid record in judo, though despite a number of bronze and silver medals, gold has proved elusive. Britain's best chance may lie with Graeme Randall, who won the under-81kg competition at the World Championships in Birmingham last year and will be seeking to repeat that feat. Britain's other medal hope in the men's competition could be extra lightweight John Buchanan who performed well in Birmingham, reaching the last eight, but failed to get a medal in the repechage.

Britain has more chance of medal success in the women's competition. Nik Fairbrother, while not at her best in the World Championships, has a good record in the under-57kg event. Karen Roberts won a World Championship medal in the under-63kg division and could repeat this in Sydney. Karina Bryant, who won bronze in Birmingham, is one to look out for in the women's heavyweight division. However, our best hope of gold may lie with Kate Howey, world champion in the under-70kg event in 1998 and runner-up last year.

Of the other nations, Japan are always strong, particularly in the men's event, as are Korea, Germany, France and Russia. Cuba are strong in the women's event.

DID YOU **KNOW?**

- Contestants must be clean, have dry skin and have cut their finger and toenails before a bout. Since opponents spend the entire bout grappling with each other at close quarters, offensive body odour is also banned.

- Making rude gestures at an opponent is banned.

- Training for judo can be unusual. In 1988, the South Korean team made early morning visits to cemeteries for solitude before going back to study videos of their opponents. It worked, as they went on to capture gold in the extra lightweight and half lightweight divisions.

JARGON BUSTER

Chui: A serious infringement equal to an award of yuko to the opponent. Any equivalent or lower penalty given to a player who has a chui increases it to a keikoku.

Fusen gachi: A win gained by default – opponent does not appear.

Grabbing inside: When a judoka grabs an opponent's jacket or pants.

Hansoku mate: A grave infringement of the rules, penalized by awarding an ippon to the opponent, which ends the match.

Hiki wake: A draw.

Ippon: A full win.

Judogi: The judoka's uniform. Consists of a baggy white/off-white jacket and loose-fitting trousers. The jacket is tied together with an 'obi'.

Judoka: A judo contestant.

Keikoku: A grave infringement equal to an award of waza-ari to the opponent. Any other penalty of any kind imposed on a player with a keikoku causes a hansoku mate and ends the match.

Kiken gachi: A win gained by an opponent's withdrawal during a match.

Koka: A near yuko. Kokas cannot be added together to make a higher score such as a yuko.

Non-combativity: The delay of activity or fighting by a judoka.

Shido: A slight infringement equal to an award of koka to the opponent. Any equivalent penalty given to a player who has a shido increases it to a chui.

Sogo gachi: A compound win. This happens when one player has gained a waza-ari and the opponent is, or has been, penalized with a keikoku.

Tatami: The rectangular competition area. Tatamis are usually made of pressed foam and measure 16 square metres in area.

Waza-ari: A half-win (two end a match and equal an ippon, or full win) or compound win (see sogo gachi, above).

Waza ari awasete ippon: A win by scoring two waza-aris.

Yuko: A near waza-ari. Yukos cannot be added together to make a higher score such as waza-ari or ippon.

Yusei gachi: A win by technical superiority.

BRITISH MEDAL COUNT

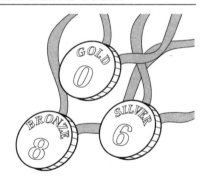

MODERN

Pentathlon

30 September – 1 October, Pavilion 2 (Shooting, Fencing);
Sydney International Aquatic Centre (Swimming);
Baseball Stadium (Showjumping, Running)

The original pentathlon, held in ancient Greece, consisted of
running the length of the Olympic stadium, throwing a spear,
jumping, throwing a discus and wrestling. When the founder of
the modern Olympics, Baron Pierre de Courbertin, saw how
successful his brainchild could be he recognized the need for
a modern version of the pentathlon to be part of the Games.
It took him until the Games of 1912 before he got his way, and
he based the 'new' event on the romantic tale of a young French
cavalry officer who had been sent on horseback to deliver a
message. Legend has it that he rode across wild terrain,
encountered enemy soldiers and fought them off with his sword.
He won a duel, only to have his horse shot while he was riding
it, forcing him to swim across a raging river and then run cross-
country in order to deliver his message. Inspired by this,
Courbertin came up with the modern pentathlon, primarily a
sport for soldiers to compete in, an event he said would 'test
a man's moral qualities as much as his physical resources and
skills, producing thereby, the ideal, complete athlete.' The sport
has not changed much since the Baron first had his dream,
though in Sydney, women will have their own competition.

The modern pentathlon is an even stiffer test than it was in 1912. In Atlanta four years ago it was decided that all five events – shooting, fencing, swimming, riding and a 3000m cross-country run – must all be completed in one gruelling 12-hour day, instead of four days. It is a formidable challenge, especially considering the sweltering heat competitors may face in Sydney. The athlete who comes out on top will have earned himself the deserved accolade as the best all-round Olympian.

WHAT TO **WATCH**

Of all the five events, only the equestrian part has altered radically since 1912. Where once it was a 5000-metre ride cross-country, competitors now jump obstacles in a stadium for the benefit of the spectators. This is an unpredictable event, even more so that it now has to be completed in one day. Positions can change at any time, particularly in the showjumping event where riders draw lots for the horses, so are riding the animal for the first time. Like the decathlon (see page 46), it is a pure test of all-round ability, adaptability and stamina.

WHAT ARE THE **RULES?**

16 athletes will contest both the women and men's events in Sydney. The athletes earn points for each of the five disciplines, with the points gained from the first four events determining the starting order for the last event, the cross-country run. The leading athlete starts first and the starting times between each of the other athletes are determined by their points difference, so that the three people who cross

the line first gain the three medals. The rules for each discipline are as follows:

Shooting – Each athlete fires 20 shots at 20 targets with a 4.5 millimetre air pistol. Each shot is fired 10 metres from the target and athletes have forty seconds to take each shot. Like archery, there are 10 rings on the target with different points value, ranging from one for the outside ring to 10 for the inner ring. Shooters must stand, fire with one hand and get just two-and-a-half minutes' practice before the competition commences. The number of points scored on the target is then converted into competition points; 172 target points (out of a maximum of 200) equals 1000 competition points. Each target point above or below that figure increases or decreases the score by 12.

Fencing – In this most ancient of duelling sports, pentathletes use an épée (see fencing, page 108) to fight each of the other competitors. Each bout lasts one minute and the first fencer to land a hit wins. If neither lands a hit, they both lose. Fencers must stop on the command of 'halt' and any hits after that command do not count. If an athlete wins 70 per cent of their bouts they score 1000 competition points, any higher or lower percentage increases or decreases the amount of points scored. Fencers are punished for dangerous play and if a person turns his back on another they receive a 10-point penalty.

Swimming – This is a 200-metre freestyle race strictly against the clock, not each other. Pentathletes are seeded into heats depending on their personal best times. A time of 2mins 30 secs (2mins 40secs for women) equals 1000 competition points. Every tenth of a second above or below these times decreases or increases the points total by one point. Two false starts, or failing to touch the end of the pool while turning, results in a 40-point penalty.

Riding – After drying themselves off, the pentathletes are split into two groups according to their current overall standings. They then draw random horses, so that the first and ninth-placed athletes ride the same horse, as do the second and tenth and so on. They all get 20 minutes to ride and get used to the horse before the competition begins. The riders have to clear 12 obstacles on the course and finish within a specific time limit, usually between one minute and one minute and 20 seconds. Each athlete begins with 1100 competition points and loses points for penalties, which include three points for every second more than the time limit, 30 points for hitting an obstacle while jumping, 60 points for falling off the horse, or if the horse falls to the ground, and 40 points if the horse refuses to jump an obstacle or runs off the course. If the horse or rider falls twice then the athlete is eliminated and if a horse refuses at the same jump three times then the rider must move on to the next obstacle.

Running – The leader runs first with all the others starting behind him/her at intervals determined by their points score. The race is 3000m long. The first person to cross the line wins gold.

WHO WILL **WIN?**

Whoever copes best with the Sydney heat has the best chance. Britain's best medal hope lies with Kate Allenby in the women's event, who will be hoping to do well after winning the world title in 1998, and finishing third in last year's World

Championships. She has a great chance but Poland's Paulina Boenisz and Anna Sulima will be very hard to beat, as will Italy's Fabiana Fares.

In the men's competition the hot favourite is Lithuanian star Andrejus Zadneprovskis. His main rivals are defending champion Alexander Parygin of Kazakhstan and Dmitri Svatkovsky of Russia.

DID YOU **KNOW?**

- One of the most illustrious of past modern pentathletes was the great military leader General George S. Patton, who represented the USA in Stockholm in 1912 and finished fifth. He could have won but was found lacking in the pistol shooting – put simply, he couldn't shoot.

- The sport produced the first Olympic athlete to fail a drug test, in Mexico in 1968. Hans Gunnar Liljenvall tested over the blood-alcohol limit. His excuse? He'd needed a few beers to calm his nerves prior to the pistol shooting.

- Eight years later and more disgrace. Boris Onishchenko was disqualified for rigging his épée during the fencing event, thus earning himself the nickname Boris Disonishchenko. Hilarious.

- The team leader for the USA in 1996 was the actor Dolph Lundgren, who played Rocky's monosyllabic Russian opponent in the film *Rocky IV*.

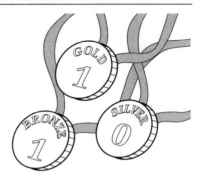

Rowing

17 – 24 September, Sydney International Regatta Centre

The man dubbed 'The Athlete of the Century' is back and attempting to make his mark in the new century. Steve Redgrave, Britain's greatest ever Olympian, is going for gold at the age of 38, but this time in a new event. His previous four gold medals have come in the coxless pairs (two self-steering oarsmen). Now, however, he is seeking his fifth in the coxless fours (four self-steering oarsmen), and will have to beat off a concerted challenge from an Australian crew who will be backed by an expected 40,000 people at the Penrith Lakes in Sydney. It promises to be the most anticipated and intriguing clash of the whole Games. Can he do it?

Rowing is one of the most popular of Olympic sports with Britons perhaps because they tend to do well in it. However, it is a massive test of endurance from beginning to end, with some crews achieving speeds of over 22mph. Britain has an illustrious history in the sport. Modern racing began on the Thames in London in the early eighteenth century with rowers racing each other for cash. The University Boat Race between Oxford and Cambridge, a British institution, began way back in 1829, with the American universities following suit 23 years later. The sport never made the first Olympics due to rough weather, but did make its debut in Paris in 1900 with five events, all held on the river Seine. The British, like in many sports, dominated the early years but the balance of power swung towards the United States and the eastern European countries in the middle of the twentieth century. In 1976, women's rowing was added, though Britain is still to win a medal in that event.

Rowing is a sport that has over the years increasingly embraced new technology. One of the major innovations was the introduction of rollers on seats, allowing rowers to lengthen their stroke and use more leg power. Now, boats are lightweight and streamlined, designed to scythe through the water at surprising speeds.

WHAT TO **WATCH**

Rowing is one of the few sports where the athletes face backwards to race, unlike canoeists, who face forwards. There are two different types of rowing, scull rowing (each rower uses two oars) and sweep rowing (each rower uses only one). So, for example, Steve Redgrave rows with one oar, and is therefore a sweep rower. The 'shaft' of a sweep oar is between 12 and 13 feet long, while the shaft of a scull oar is around 10 feet long. The blade of a sweep is bigger than the scull, though they still have the same curved shape.

In the Olympics there are eight men's events and six women's. The men's events are single scull, double (two-rower) scull, lightweight double scull, quadruple scull, coxless pair, coxless four, lightweight coxless four and coxed eight. The women's events are single scull, double scull, lightweight double scull, quadruple scull, coxless pair and coxed eight.

Coxless refers to the fact that the crew row without a cox to guide them.

Coxes navigate for the rowers. They are the only person facing forwards and who can see where the boat is going. They will also call the 'stroke', determining the rowers' rhythm, and keep their eye on the opposition. Boats without a cox, or coxswain to give them their full title, are sometimes referred to as 'blind boats'.

A stroke has four components that have to be completed perfectly to propel the boat forward as fast as possible. These are:

Catch – The rower drops the oar into the water with the body coiled forwards, arms at full stretch.

Drive – The legs power the seat back as the rower uncoils, drawing the oar against the water as the legs stretch fully out and arms pull into the body.

Finish – The rower lifts the oar out of the water and rolls it to a horizontal position so the blade slices through the air aerodynamically for the final component of the stroke which is:

Recovery – The rower slides forwards, back into the coiled position, arms outstretched, ready for the next catch.

The ability to synchronize these strokes as perfectly as possible is the key in achieving maximum speed. If one crew member loses rhythm, even slightly, it can ruin a team's race. Rowers who are not rowing well will create a lot of splash around the area where the oar hits the water. At amateur level, this can cause an oar to be lost or even overturn the whole boat. However, this is unlikely to happen at Olympic level.

In sweep rowing events, the second rower from the cox is vital. The first rower from the cox is in the 'stroke' seat, they set the pace for the rest to follow. But if the second rower, whose oar is at the other side, does not match the stroke then the whole of his side will be out of synch, a disaster for any crew. The more crew members, the faster the boat. A crew of eight will average around 40 to 44 strokes per minute, while a single scull will manage 36 to 40 strokes at the start of a race. The start is vital. Rowing is one of the few sports where athletes will give their all to begin with to get a lead and so row in clear, flat water. In the main body of the race the stroke will drop the stroke rate as a rhythm is established, but increase it for the final sprint to the line.

WHAT ARE THE **RULES?**

The Sydney course is man-made but like all rowing courses is 2000 metres long. The course is divided into nine lanes, though rowing rules do not actually state that rowers must stay in a particular lane. The only dictate is that they must not interfere with another crew. In reality, though, they do stay in lanes because the shortest route between two points is a straight line.

The field for the final in each event is determined by a series of heats, semi-finals and repechages (repechages give losing boats a second chance to get to the semi-final). The first three teams in each semi-final move through to the six-lane final, though this does depend on the number of boats entered into each event.

Rules to note include:

- The cox must weigh at least 55kg in men's events and 50kg in women's events. If they are lighter a dead weight can be added to make up the difference.

- The cox is counted as a member of the crew, so it means a man cannot steer a boat in the women's competition and vice versa.

- A crew can continue to race if a rower falls overboard, but cannot if the cox (if there is one) falls overboard.

- A race can be stopped if a boat suffers a mechanical breakdown within the first 100 metres.

WHO WILL **WIN?**

The clash everyone is waiting for is between the British and Australian men's coxless fours, who are known as the 'Oarsome Foursome'. Steve Redgrave is joined by his 1996 gold medal-winning partner, Matthew Pinsent, together with two from James Cracknell, Ed Coode and Tim Foster. Throughout 1999, the team were unstoppable, remaining unbeaten and claiming the World Championship gold beating the Australians in the final. However, a new Australian four has been formed, but only time will tell if they are strong enough to give the British a good race.

Great Britain also has medal hopes in the men's eight. Led by Tim Foster, and featuring Rob Thatcher, Ben Hunt-Davies, Fred Scarlett, Louis Atrill, Luka Grubor, Kieran West, Steve Trapmere and cox Rowley Douglas, the eight just missed on World Championship glory when they were pipped on the line by the USA. They will be seeking revenge, and should at least get a medal.

The British have a chance to break their medal duck in the women's event as well, though it will be tough. Dot Blackie and Cath Bishop will have to improve upon their excellent fifth in the World Championships, but informed opinion believes they are capable of it.

In Atlanta, Australia took the most gold medals and could do so again, though they will be challenged by the USA, Italy, Germany, Canada and the Netherlands, who will all field strong crews.

DID YOU **KNOW?**

- Dieticians recommend that top rowers should consume around 6000 calories a day to maintain their energy levels.

- Before the invention of the sliding seat, rowers used to grease their pants and apply oatmeal on the seat to enable them to slide back and forth.

- The point when a rowing boat is moving at its fastest is not when the oars are in the water. Maximum speed is achieved when the rowers slide back towards their feet and recoil. The oars, meanwhile, are in the air.

- Dr Spock (not the *Star Trek* character),the author of the American childcare classic *Dr Spock's Baby and Childcare Book*, rowed in the USA's gold-winning men's eight crew at the Paris Games of 1924.

Catching a crab: Occurs when a rower is too slow in releasing his blade from the water at the end of a stroke and the oar gets pulled under. The consequent force sometimes hurls the rower from the boat or 'shell'.

Coxswain: The person who steers the shell and directs the race plan, acting as the eyes of the crew. Sometimes considered an on-the-water coach for the crew.

Feathering: Holding the blades in a horizontal position out of the water between strokes to reduce wind resistance during recovery (see page 159); one of the most difficult aspects of rowing for beginners.

Hatchet: A recent innovation in oar shape; resembles a hatchet.

Power: A call for rowers to do 10 of their best, most powerful strokes. It's a strategy used to pull ahead of a competitor.

Puddles: The water swirls left by oars during a stroke.

Stern: The rear of the boat; the direction the rowers are facing.

Straight: Refers to a shell without a coxswain.

Stretcher or Footstretcher: Where the rowers' feet are placed. The stretcher consists of two inclined footrests, which hold the rower's shoes. The rower's shoes are bolted into the footrests.

Stroke: Rower who sits closest to the stern. The stroke sets the rhythm for the boat – others behind him must follow his rhythm or 'cadence'.

Washing: A warning or foul charged against a crew which drifts from its lane and upsets another boat with churned-up water.

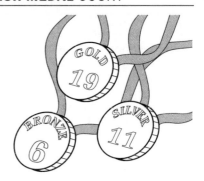

Sailing

16 – 30 September, Sydney Harbour

No other sport will have the same spectacular setting as the sailing competition. All the events will be conducted on Sydney Harbour, with the Opera House and the Harbour Bridge as a backdrop, and will have the tourist board trembling with glee. It is also good news for spectators who will actually be able to see what is going on from the foreshore. Usually, races are held out to sea and based at locations miles away from the host city.

Before this Olympics, the sport was called yachting, and Britain's ruling body is still known as the Royal Yachting Association, but the name has now been changed. Marketing in modern sport is everything, and the organizers thought that not only was the word 'yachting' too old-fashioned, but that people believed the sport was only for the rich upper-classes.

Sailing as a sport had its first international competition in 1851 with a small 60-mile race around the Isle of Wight named the Hundred Guineas Cup. It was won by an American yacht which returned across the Atlantic with the trophy. This trophy was renamed the America's Cup and was held by the

USA until their crew was eventually defeated in 1983, the end of an amazing 132-year winning streak.

The sport first featured in the 1900 Games, after bad weather prevented it from being part of the inaugural Games four years earlier. In the early days, if you had the best boat, you would win. Now, however, boats race in classes of similar designs so that skill, rather than craftsmanship, is rewarded.

WHAT TO **WATCH**

There are nine different classes of boats and 11 sailing events. The different classes can be arranged into four different types. These are:

- Mistral – This is a type of windsurfer, consisting of a board with a mast and a sail. The sailor controls the mast with their arms and steers in a standing position, moving their body weight to guide the vessel. Men and women have their own mistral event.

- Dinghy – Finn, Europe, Laser, 49er and 470 classes are all dinghies. The Finn, Europe and Laser have a single sail, while the 470 class has a two-sail rig. 470s and the 49ers also have an additional sail for heading downwind, called a spinnaker. Sailors steer dinghies using a rudder and the crew use their body weight to counterbalance the sideways forces developed by the sail. At the Olympics, the Finn is used only in men's events and the Europe used only in women's. The 470 has both men's and women's events, while the Laser and 49ers are open events (i.e., both men and women may enter).

- Keelboats – The Soling and Star classes are both keelboats. Keelboats, as the name implies, have a keel fixed below the hull, while the Soling also has a spinnaker. Soling and Star are both open events at the Games.

- Catamarans – These are twin-hulled boats with a centreboard and a rudder on each hull, a two-sail rig and a mainsail. The only catamaran event in Sydney will be the Tornado, an open event.

The different types of boats require sailors of differing physiques to get the best performance out of them. The Finn class, for example, is likely to have tall, heavy men sailing them, whilst 470 sailors tend to be much lighter. The Mistral, Laser, Europe and Finn are all single-handed events, while the 470, Star, 49er, and Tornado are all double-handed. The only triple-handed event is the Soling.

One further thing to note is that no boat is able to sail directly into the wind and move forwards. Therefore, when facing upwind, sailors employ a technique known as 'tacking', which involves sailing in a zig-zag pattern, 45 degrees to the left, then 45 degrees to the right.

WHAT ARE THE **RULES?**

There are two types of racing, fleet racing and match racing. In match racing, which applies only in the Soling class, competitors race boat against boat. Each competitor tries to manoeuvre the other into making an error or violating the rules, which incurs penalties. These races are held on much shorter courses than fleet races. The Soling boats compete in a fleet race (see below) to decide seedings, and then in a match-racing round robin (where each competitor races

173

against each other). The leading boats progress through to another round of match racing, and the top boats from that round go forward to the finals where the medals are decided.

Fleet racing runs on the principle that the first boat to cross the line wins the race. In all fleet events there are a series of 11 races, except for the 49er which has 16. Boats are awarded points according to where they finished in each race. First place gets one point, the second gets two points and so on. After five races each boat discards its worst result, and after nine races, the worst two are discarded. The winner is the boat with the lowest accumulated score at the end of the race series.

During a race, there are strict rules governing how boats can move among each other. Boats that contravene right-of-way rules can avoid punishment if they voluntarily sail in two circles; this penalty is known as a 720. In the Tornado and 49ers class, boats are only required to sail one circle – a 360. Boats that do not sail circles voluntarily run the risk of disqualification at the end of a race, unless they can convince the judges otherwise. The basic right-of-way rules are:

- When two boats on opposite tacks meet, the onus is on the port-tack boat to stay clear of the starboard-tack boat.

- When two boats on the same tack overlap (or are more or less side by side) the boat closest the wind must stay clear.

A competitor who feels he has been unfairly treated by another boat in the race can protest to the judges within 90 minutes of the end of the race. Five judges hear the protest, with other competitors appearing as witnesses for either side.

The two types of courses used are called windward return and trapezoidal. A windward return course, obligatory for 49-ers and Tornadoes, requires boats to sail against the wind to one mark, then return with the wind to a second mark. A trapezoidal layout is a four-leg course with separate starting and finish lines. The end of each leg is marked with a buoy, which boats must avoid, or face being penalized with a 360. A leg sailing against the wind (windward) is known as a beat, sailing with the wind (leeward) is named a run. If the wind is neither with or against the leg is called a reach.

WHO WILL **WIN?**

Traditionally, Great Britain has always done well in the sailing events. This year, the British have one of our best gold medal hopes of the whole Games in the shape of the remarkable Ben Ainslie. He won silver in the Laser class in Atlanta aged just 19, and since then he has not looked back. 1999 was a fabulous year and at the time of writing he was world, European, national, Asia-Pacific and pre-Olympic champion and was voted Yachtsman of the Year in 1999. The only thing missing from his trophy collection is the gold medal and there is every chance he will win it.

Another gold medal hope is in the Finn class, with European champion Iain Percy, who is only one year older than Ainslie. That European performance prompted team manager John Derbyshire to proclaim Percy as a genuine gold medal contender, a fact the sailor backed up when he won gold at the pre-Olympic regatta in Sydney last January. Of the women, Shirley Robertson has a superb chance of winning a medal in the Europe class. Last year she won silver in the European Championships which she followed up with the same performance at the World Championships in Brazil.

Other British medal hopes include Ian Walker (who won silver in Atlanta in 1996 with the late John Merricks) and Mark Covell in the Star class, Nick Rogers and Joe Glanfield in the 470, and Rob Wilson and Will Howden in the Tornado. All of them will meet strong competition from sailors from the USA, Norway, Sweden, Denmark, and the hosts Australia, who won the most medals in 1996 and possess local knowledge of the elements.

DID YOU **KNOW?**

- The fastest boat is the Tornado which can reach speeds of more than 30mph.

- In the sailing competition of the 1908 Olympics one of the more unusual events was motorboat racing. It has not reappeared since.

- In 1988 at Seoul, Canadian Lawrence Lemieux left the course in his boat to rescue a sailor who was being swept away to sea after his boat had capsized. He won a special award for his endeavours.

Beating: Sailing (or pointing) at an angle into the wind or upwind – also known as tacking. Since sailboats cannot sail directly into the wind, 'beating' is the closest course to the wind they can sail.

Blanketing: A tactical manoeuvre in which one boat slows a competitor by positioning itself to stop the wind reaching the competitor's sails.

Broach: Occurs in a downwind situation, when the boat is pushed by the wind onto its side, so the mast is parallel to the water. As a rule, the boat will right itself.

Centreboard: Like a keel, a centreboard is a weighted appendage attached to the bottom of the boat to keep it from capsizing. It also supplies the force that

enables the boat to sail upwind. Unlike a keel, it is retractable.

Fall off: A manoeuvre in which a boat turns away from the wind.

Helmsman: The crew member, usually the skipper (captain), who steers the boat. Also called the 'driver'.

Hiking out: Leaning off the side of the craft to change the centre of gravity of the boat and go faster.

Hiking straps: Straps attached to the feet that help a sailor hike out more, minimizing the chance of falling out of the boat.

Keel: A weighted, non-moveable appendage attached to the bottom of the boat that keeps it from capsizing and also supplies the force that enables the boat to sail upwind.

Knot: One nautical mile per hour.

Off the wind: Sailing away from the wind; also downwind, reaching or running (see page 169).

Spinnaker: Large, light ballooning sails that are only attached to the corners. They are used when running or reaching, sailing downwind (see page 169).

Tiller: A lever used to turn the steering rudder of a boat from side to side.

BRITISH MEDAL COUNT

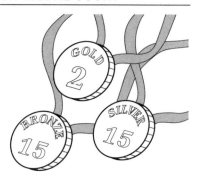

Shooting

16 – 23 September, Sydney International Shooting Centre

The size of the Olympic shooting event has grown immensely over the years. In 1896, there were just three events. Now there are 17 gold medals to be contested, a testament to the sport's growing popularity. It is a sport that tests the nerves of even the steeliest competitor, and requires much more than just a steady hand and a good eye. All of those participating in Sydney are excellent shots but it is the ones who can keep their nerve under massive amounts of pressure who will walk away with the top prizes. Many of the targets are hardly visible to the naked eye and look no bigger than the eye of a needle, so the slightest distraction can cost points. Stories abound of shooters firing between heartbeats to avoid disruption, and many wear stiff, thick jackets not only to provide support, but also to muffle the pulse of the heart. Intense concentration is vital at all times.

Of course, the origins of shooting goes back centuries, to the time of muskets and muzzle-loading weapons. It first entered the Olympics in 1896 when the Games' founder, Baron Pierre de Coubertin, a former French pistol champion, insisted his favoured sport was included. Since that time it has only been left out of two Olympics, in 1904 and 1928, and although team events have been dropped, skeet shooting (see below) has been added. Women participate in seven shooting events of their own; before 1984, all events were open to both men and women and up until 1992 the trap (see below) and skeet were still open. Improvements in technology and firearms have caused a growth in the number of events, so that in Sydney, a total of 410 shooters are expected to compete, making it one of the Games' largest sports.

WHAT TO **WATCH**

Of the 17 events, six are contested with shotguns, five with pistols and six with rifles. The most exciting events to watch are those with moving targets, which the shooter must hit within a time limit. Here is a short dossier of each event, divided according to weapon:

Shotgun

In the trap, double trap and skeet competitions, shooters stand in shooting stations firing at clay targets (clay pigeons) which are released and fly through the air upon the call of 'pull!' from the shooter. The person who hits the most targets wins.

- **Trap** – This is named after the device that fires the clay target. One of three traps at differing heights and angles fires a target – the shooter does not know which – and the competitor is allowed two shots at it before it hits the ground. A target's speed through the air can reach 75mph.

- **Double Trap** – Two targets are released simultaneously at different heights and angles from two of three traps, ranging in height from three to three and a half metres. The shooter must fire just one shot at each target.

- **Skeet** – Targets take off at different heights and at opposite sides of the range. The two traps are arranged in a semi-circle, and throw out either 'single' or 'double' targets. A single target can be thrown from either trap. A double target comprises two targets thrown simultaneously, one from each trap. Skeet shooters can fire just one shot at each target and cannot raise the gun from their waist until the targets are released.

Rifle

Rifle events are held on shooting ranges where competitors shoot at targets at distances of 10, 25 and 50 metres. A running target event has shooters firing at a moving target from a distance of 10 metres as it moves across a two-metre opening in front of them. For the running target competition, the shooter stands, and cannot support his left arm (or right arm if the shooter is left-handed) on his hip or chest. In the standing position for all other rifle events, such support is allowed.

In the kneeling position, used in the three-position rifle competition, the shooter, if right-handed, may touch the ground with the toe of the right foot, the right knee and the left foot. The left knee is allowed to support the elbow, and vice versa for left-handers. The other two positions used in the three-position rifle competition are standing and prone.

In the prone position, also used in the free rifle prone competition, a shooter cannot rest the rifle on any object.

Pistol

Pistol shooters shoot at targets from distances of 10, 25 and 50 metres. They can only use one hand to fire the pistol.

WHAT ARE **THE RULES?**

Electronic targets are used in rifle and pistol events. All the targets have ten concentric rings with different points value, the inner ring being the bullseye and normally worth 10 points, the outer ring normally being worth one. The shooter with the most points at the end wins. Rules vary when a shot breaks the line between two rings. The higher score is generally awarded, though in air rifle competitions the 10 ring, or the bullseye, must be shot out completely to score a perfect 10.

In shotgun and running target events the shooter who hits the highest number of targets wins the competition.

Other rules to note include:

- In shotgun, the referee has the final say on whether a target has been hit or not. A target is declared 'hit' when at least one visible piece has been broken from it.

- In shotgun, a tied final is decided by a shoot-off, and the first person to miss a target is eliminated.

- Shooters may participate in more than one event at the Olympics provided they have met the criteria for qualification in that event.

WHO WILL **WIN?**

The Europeans dominate shooting. Great Britain has had some success in the past and has a few medal hopes. The best is probably Richard Faulds, a former world record holder, in the double trap. The other British medal hope is Drew Harvey in the skeet. He was a junior world champion in 1998 and a silver medallist in the skeet during the 1999 World

Championships. Mike Babb in the smallbore prone rifle is the other shooter gunning for glory. The most likely gold medallists are from eastern Europe, especially Russia where the men dominate the rifle and pistol events, while Australia and Italy always fare well in the shotgun events. The eastern Europeans also dominate the women's event, though China's Shan Zhan will be hoping to win the women's new skeet competition. She won the open event at Barcelona in 1992 but did not have the chance to defend in Atlanta because the skeet was made a men-only event. The men's star performer is German Ralf Schumann, who is going for his third consecutive gold in the 25-metre rapid-fire pistol event, which would be an Olympic shooting record.

DID YOU **KNOW?**

- Hungary's Karoly Takacs won two golds in the rapid-fire pistol event in 1948, just 10 years after a hand grenade exploded in his right hand and blew it off. He taught himself to shoot left-handed – and did it pretty well.

- In 1980 another Hungarian, Karoly Varga, won the prone rifle event with a broken shooting hand. He later told the media that it helped him win, as it forced him to squeeze the trigger in a lighter fashion than usual.

- In the 1900 Olympics, live pigeons were used as targets. It only happened once.

- In 1908 in London, the Russian Military Rifle Team turned up for the event 12 days late. The Russians used the Gregorian calendar, which has different dates to ours, and so missed the event.

JARGON BUSTER

Airgun: A rifle or pistol that uses compressed air or carbon dioxide to discharge metallic pellets.

Bore: The interior diameter of a gun barrel.

Bunker: In trap shooting, the underground 'dugout' in front of the competitors' firing line from which traps throw clay targets.

Calibre: The interior diameter of a rifle or pistol barrel.

Crossfire: A shot accidentally fired at a target assigned to another competitor.

Firing line: The line from which competitors position themselves to shoot their targets.

Sighters: Practice shots fired at the beginning of a match to check sight adjustments.

String: A series of shots, normally five or 10.

Ten-ring: The innermost ring of the black section of a target.

BRITISH MEDAL COUNT

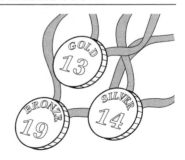

Softball

In Olympic terms, softball can be described as a baseball event for women. It was introduced in the 1996 Olympics in Atlanta, though cynics said it was simply to guarantee the USA yet another gold medal. However, the competition in Atlanta proved a success with both the paying public and TV viewers because the matches were played with great intensity. And now it looks as if Australia might challenge America's superiority, too.

Softball in Britain is often a gentle, social, summertime game played by office workers in parks. Olympic softball is not quite so genteel. Its full title is fast-pitch softball, amply illustrated in Atlanta when one pitch was clocked at 118kph, which, considering the distance between pitcher and batter is just 40 feet, 20 feet less than baseball, is frightening. In fact, at such speed, a softball batter has less time to react than a baseball player.

The history of softball comes with one of those sporting myths so beloved by Americans. Apparently, a Yale graduate was celebrating his college's victory over rivals Harvard, and did so, bizarrely, by throwing a boxing glove at a Harvard man while at a boating club in Chicago. The Harvard man, his name lost in the mists of time, hit the glove away with a stick. An idea formed in both men's heads, and shortly the glove became a big ball, the stick a big, long bat and softball was born. Since 1965, a World Championship has been held and 110 countries are now affiliated to the International Softball Federation.

WHAT TO **WATCH**

Of course, softball bears a striking resemblance to baseball. However, there are several crucial differences, which are:

- The ball is bigger.

- The bat is bigger.

- The pitch is smaller. In softball, the bases are 60 feet apart, compared to 90 feet in baseball.

- The pitching distance is 40 feet in softball, compared to 60 feet in baseball.

- Pitchers release the ball underarm rather than overarm.

- There is no pitchers mound.

- Runners on a base in softball must keep one foot on the base until the pitcher has released the ball.

- The game is only seven innings, two less than baseball.

- Softball is played on a dirt infield, while baseball is played on a grass one.

Other minor differences include a 'safety base' in softball. This is at first base and is an orange base attached to the normal white one. The runner must run to the orange base, while the baseman must touch the white one. This helps avoid collisions that can occur when runners are sprinting and diving to first base. Softball also allows players to use three-sided bats, though not many do.

WHAT ARE THE **RULES?**

Bearing in mind the differences outlined above, readers are referred to the rules in the baseball section. The competition will involve eight teams competing in a single pool. The eight are Australia, USA, Japan, Canada, China, Italy, New Zealand and Cuba. Each side plays each other once, with the top four advancing to contest the semi-finals. The top team will play the second placed team with the winners going through to the Grand Final. The loser of the match between the first and second-placed teams from the pool, plays the winner between the third and fourth-placed teams. The loser of that contest wins the bronze, while the winner goes forward to play in the final.

If a match is tied after seven innings, then the teams play another innings, one at a time until one side wins. If it is still tied after nine innings each team starts their turn at batting with a runner on second base to increase their chances of scoring.

WHO WILL **WIN?**

The USA are still favourites, but Australia are now strong challengers. The only game the USA lost in Atlanta in 1996 was to Australia, and the 'Wallabies' repeated that feat during the 1998 World Championships, winning 2–1, though the

USA gained revenge with a tight 1–0 victory in the final. Those two sides will battle out the gold. Everyone else will play for bronze. Japan, 1996 Olympic silver medallists China, and Canada should be the main contenders for third place with New Zealand, Cuba and the only European entrant, Italy, there to make up the numbers. The game's star player is American Lisa Fernandez, the world's best pitcher and one of the reasons why the Americans have dominated the game, though Australia's Tanya Harding could challenge her reputation as the world's best.

DID YOU **KNOW?**

- Softball is America's biggest recreational sport, played by more than 40 million people.

- A softball is three inches bigger in circumference than a baseball.

- In ten years of competition between 1986 and 1996, the United States lost only one match – and won 110.

- That record was broken in the most dramatic circumstances in 1996. The US were 1–0 up in the tenth innings, two people were out and Australian batter Joanne Brown had two strikes against her name. Amazingly she struck a home run, with a player already on a base, to win the match 2–1.

Swimming

16 – 23 September, Sydney International Aquatic Centre

Everyone involved with swimming will hope that the event in Sydney will pass off without being tainted by rumours of drug misuse. Unfortunately, innuendo, smears and the general feeling that something is not right have marred the last two Games. This harked back to the bad old days of the 1970s when each medal winner from the former East German team was treated with suspicion, a feeling confirmed in the early 1990s when former East German officials admitted administering steroids to their team. In 1992, the Chinese women burst onto the international stage and won a surprising four gold medals. Everyone's unease was compounded when they won 12 of the 16 events in the 1994 World Championships. People whispered, pointed fingers and noted that the men, who with naturally high levels of testosterone would not have benefited so much from taking the steroids, failed to make the same impact as the women. Twelve Chinese women failed drug tests in 1994 alone, several of them caught by their own officials. Since a crackdown both on behalf of FINA, the international swimming federation, and the Chinese themselves, the performance of Chinese women is less spectacular and there is a feeling that a level playing field has been re-established.

In 1996, the unease was not so widespread, but the whispering campaign got underway when Ireland's Michelle Smith de Bruin won three gold medals, drastically improving her personal best times in the process. To stop this damage to the sport's reputation, FINA have got tough, increasing drug tests both in and out of competition, and increasing the ban from international competition for use of steroids to four years. With these regulations in place there has been a marked drop in the amount of swimmers banned for drug abuse, and the view is the problem is almost under control. There will always be a few performers who slip through the net, but in Sydney we should be seeing the fastest natural swimmers on Earth.

Controversy aside, swimming has always been one of the most thrilling and eagerly anticipated sports in the Olympics. It is the first 'big' event of the Games, where the most medals are won before the track and field events get underway. In Australia, where swimmers are idolized, expect a tremendous atmosphere, as fans flock to see their hyped home favourites. Expect some very tight races, tumbling world records and get used to the sound of the Australian national anthem.

The sport was part of the first Games in 1896 in Athens, when the 1200-metre freestyle event involved a boat dropping the swimmers in the Mediterranean and required them to swim back to shore in icy waters. Survival mattered more than swimming. Things weren't much better four years later at the Paris Games, when races took place in the waters of the River Seine. One of the events, bizarrely, was an obstacle race on water. At the 1908 games in London, a swimming pool was constructed in the middle of the athletics stadium. Four years later, women started competing in the Games, and since that point the event has never looked back. It is now established as one of the Games' 'glory' sports.

WHAT TO **WATCH**

Swimmers compete in four different strokes: 'freestyle' (though see below), breaststroke, backstroke and the butterfly. The quickest times come in the freestyle, using the front crawl, while the slowest come in the breaststroke. Here is short guide to each one:

Freestyle
Freestyle is not actually a stroke. In this event, swimmers can pick whatever stroke they wish, but the reality is that they always pick the fastest one, the crawl. However, in the 'medley' event, where racers compete using all four strokes, the freestyle leg must be swum using the crawl. During the freestyle event, some part of the body must be above the surface of the water at all times, apart from 15 metres after a start or a turn when competitors may swim underwater.

Breaststroke
Swimmers must swim face down moving their arms and legs together in a horizontal movement. While underwater at the start and the turn, swimmers are only allowed to make one arm stroke and one leg kick.

During the race the swimmer's head can be immersed completely, but must break the surface of the water during every complete stroke. Swimmers must touch the end of the pool with both hands.

Backstroke

This is the only race where competitors start in the water. As the name suggest, they must swim on their backs, although they can rotate their body to some degree as they swim. Once again, swimmers can only spend 15 metres underwater after a start or turn.

Butterfly

This is probably the most physically demanding of all the strokes. It apparently evolved from a loophole in the breaststroke laws. It differs from the latter in that the arms and legs move vertically rather than horizontally. Swimmers must swim face down and on the surface of the water, apart from the 15 metres after each start and turn. At each turn and at the end of a race, the swimmers must touch the end of the pool with both hands. The arms and feet must move together during a stroke.

Swimmers swim in lanes, usually eight, with the fastest ones racing in the middle lanes. However, in a final, this does not mean that the swimmers in lanes four and five are certain to win. Quite often, due to the number of heats and, for the first time in the Olympics, a semi-final stage, the faster competitors will conserve their energy for the final, so may not have the fastest qualifying times and therefore will not be in the middle lanes.

WHAT ARE THE **RULES?**

Men and women compete in 16 events each in a 50-metre-long pool. The events are identical apart from the men's 1500m freestyle and the women's 800m freestyle. Individual medley events are held over 200m and 400m, with the competitors using all four strokes in each leg in a set order – butterfly, backstroke, breaststroke and freestyle. In the medley relay a different swimmer swims each leg using a particular stroke, in a different order – backstroke, breaststroke, butterfly and freestyle.

For turning, freestyle and backstroke swimmers can use any parts of their body to touch the end of the pool, allowing them to 'tumble turn', so using their feet to kick off powerfully for the next lap. They can also finish by touching with one hand.

Butterfly and breaststroke competitors must touch the end with both hands. The only exception is in the medley when swimmers switch from backstroke to breaststroke. They must keep on their backs until they touch the end of the pool.

Other rules include:

- A swimmer is disqualified for a false start in any race.

- An electronic system decides false starts and determines exactly when swimmers touch the end of the pool when a race finishes.

- A relay team is disqualified if any member of the team takes off more than 0.3 seconds before a team member touches the end of the pool.

In Sydney, each race has a maximum of eight swimmers. There are preliminary heats in races over 50m, 100m and 200m that lead to semi-finals and then finals, all based on who gains the fastest times. In the relays and all other individual events the eight fastest finishers in the preliminary heats advance straight through to the finals.

WHO WILL **WIN?**

The pool competition promises to be thrilling – and more open than ever. In the past, the USA and Russia have dominated, but swimmers from all over the globe are now establishing themselves. Australia, in front of a noisy home crowd, are expected to do well, and head the medal table at the end. In world record holders Ian Thorpe and Susie O'Neill they have two of the possible stars of the pool. Both could take two gold medals in their individual events, not counting the relays, and Thorpe could even make it three. He is a hot favourite for the men's 200m and 400m freestyle, and has threatened to compete in the 1500m, though his compatriot Grant Hackett may not want him to. Other names to watch include the Netherlands' Pieter van der Hoogenband and South Africa's Penelope Heyns, who will also be searching for two gold medals in their chosen events. However, for Britain, it promises to be a meagre Olympics. Sue Rolph is our best chance of success in the 50m freestyle, while both Paul Palmer, in the 200m freestyle, and James Hickman, in the 100m and 200m butterfly, have only outside chances of a medal. For the rest, simply reaching the final would be a massive achievement.

Here is a short guide to each event with medal predictions, compiled with the help of the Amateur Swimming Association of Great Britain, based on 1999 form in the European Championships, the Pan American Championships and the African Championships. It does not take into account world rankings, only achievements in major championships when the pressure is at its highest. World record times given were correct at 31 January 2000, and so could have changed in the run-up to the Games. Where Britain has a slim hope of a medal, it has been indicated.

50m Freestyle, men
Tom Jager (USA)
1990, 21.81secs
1. Pieter van der Hoogenband NED
2. Brendon Dedekind RSA   3. Lorenzo Vismara ITA

50m Freestyle, women
Jingyi Le (CHN)
1994, 24.51secs
1. Inge de Bruijn NED
2. Therese Alshammar SWE   3. Tammie Spatz USA
British Medal Hope: Sue Rolph

100m Freestyle, men
Alexander Popov (RUS)
1994, 48.21secs
1. Pieter van der Hoogenband NED
2. Alexander Popov RUS   3. Michael Klim AUS

100m Freestyle, women
Jingyi Lee (CHN)
1994, 54.01secs
1. Jenny Thompson USA
2. Sue Rolph GBR   3. Sarah Ryan AUS

200m Freestyle, men
Ian Thorpe (AUS)
2000, 1min 46.00secs
1. Ian Thorpe AUS
2. Pieter van der Hoogenband NED
3. Michael Klim, AUS
British Medal Hope: Paul Palmer

200m Freestyle, women   Franziska van Almsick (GER)
1994, 1min 56.78secs
1. Susan O'Neill AUS
2. Camelia Potec ROM   3. Lindsay Benko USA

400m Freestyle, men Ian Thorpe (AUS)
1999, 3mins 41.83secs
1. Ian Thorpe AUS
2. Grant Hackett AUS 3. Ryk Neethling RSA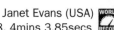
British Medal Hope: Paul Palmer

400m Freestyle, women Janet Evans (USA)
1988, 4mins 3.85secs
1. Camelia Potec ROM
2. Brooke Bennett USA 3. Kerstin Kielglass GER

1500m Freestyle, men Kieran Perkins (AUS)
1994, 14mins 41.66secs
1. Grant Hackett AUS
2. Ryk Neethling RSA 3. Chris Thompson USA
British Medal Hope: Graeme Smith

800m Freestyle, women Janet Evans (USA)
1989, 8mins 16.22secs
1. Brooke Bennett USA
2. Rachel Harris AUS 3. Hannah Stockbauer GER

100m Backstroke, men Lenny Krayzelburg (USA)
1999, 53.60secs
1. Lenny Krayzelburg USA
2. Rodolfo Falcon CUB 3. Stev Theloke GER

100m Backstroke, women Cihong He (CHN)
1994, 1min 00.16secs
1. Sandra Volker GER
2. Mai Nakamura JPN 3. Dyana Calub AUS

200m Backstroke, men   Lenny Krayzelburg (USA)
1999, 1min 55.87secs
1. Lenny Krayzelburg USA
2. Leonardo Cosh BRA   3. Ralf Braun GER

200m Backstroke, women Krisztina Egerszegi (HUN)
1991, 2mins 06.62secs,
1. Tomoko Hagiwara JPN
2. Miki Nakao JPN   3. Roxana Maricineanu FRA

100m Breaststroke,men   Fred DeBurghgraeve (BEL)
1996, 1min 00.60secs,
1. Domenico Fioravanti ITA
2. Glenn Ed Moses USA   3. Mark Warnecke GER

100m Breaststroke, women Penelope Heyns (RSA),
1999, 1min 06.52secs
1. Penelope Heyns RSA
2. Megan Quann USA   3. Agnes Kovacs HUN

200m Breaststroke, men   Mike Barrowman (USA)
1992, 2mins 10.16secs
1. Stephan Perrot FRA
2. Dimitri Komornikov RUS   3. Yohan Bernard FRA

200m Breaststroke, women   Penelope Heyns (RSA)
1999, 2mins 23.64secs
1. Penelope Heyns RSA
2. Kristy Kowal USA   3. Sarah Poewe RSA

100m Butterfly, men   Michael Klim (AUS)
1997, 52.15secs
1. Michael Klim AUS
2. Geoff Huegill AUS   3. Lars Frolander SWE
British Medal Hope: James Hickman

100m Butterfly, women   Jenny Thompson (USA)
1999, 57.88secs
1. Jenny Thompson USA
2. Inge de Bruijn NED   3. Johanna Sjoberg SWE

200m Butterfly, men   Denis Pankratov (RUS)
1995, 1min 55.22secs
1. Tom Malchow USA
2. Takashi Yamamoto JPN   3. Franck Esposito FRA
British Medal Hope: James Hickman

200m Butterfly, women   Mary Meagher (USA)
1981, 2mins 05.96secs
1. Susan O'Neill AUS
2. Jessica Deglau CAN   3. Mette Jacobsen DEN

200m Individual Medley, men   Jani Sievinen (FIN)
1994, 1min 58.16secs
1. Tom Wilkens USA
2. Marcel Wouda NED   3. Curtis Myden CAN

200m Individual Medley, women Allison Wagner (USA)
1993, 2mins 07.79secs
1. Joanne Malar CAN
2. Jana Klochkova UKR   3. Lori Munz AUS

400m Individual Medley, men   Tom Dolan (USA)
1994, 4mins 12.30secs
1. Matthew Dunn AUS
2. Curtis Myden CAN   3. Frederik Hviid ESP

400m Individual Medley, women   Yan Chen (CHN)
1997, 4mins 34.79secs
1. Jana Klochkova UKR
2. Joanne Malar CAN   3. Yasuko Tajima JPN

4 × 100m Freestyle, men   USA
1995, 3mins 15.11secs
1. Australia
2. Netherlands   3. USA

4 × 100m Freestyle, women   CHN
1994, 3mins 37.91secs
1. Germany
2. USA   3. Australia

4 × 200m Freestyle, men   AUS
1999, 7mins 08.79secs
1. Australia
2. USA 3. Germany
British Medal Hopes: GBR

4 × 200m Freestyle, women   GER
1987, 7mins 55.47secs
1. USA
2. Australia   3. Germany

4 × 100m Medley, men   USA
                        1996, 3mins 24.84secs
                                      1. USA
                  2. Netherlands   3. Canada

4 × 100m Medley, women   CHN
                        1994, 4mins 01.67secs
                                      1. USA
                  2. Australia   3. Japan

DID YOU **KNOW?**

- In the 1900 Games, an underwater swimming event was held. With obviously limited spectator value it swiftly sank without trace before the next Olympics.

- In 1952, when Frenchman Jean Boiteux won the men's 400m freestyle, his father jumped in the pool fully-clothed complete with beret, to celebrate with him.

- Swimmers shave the hair off their entire body in order to reduce friction through the water and cut valuable tenths of seconds off their time.

- In 1976, the USA men's medley team had so many good swimmers that one relay team set a world record in the morning – then a completely different team broke it in the final.

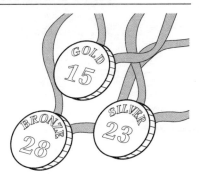

SYNCHRONIZED
Swimming

24 – 29 September, Sydney International Aquatic Centre

When synchronized swimming was finally accepted as an Olympic sport in 1984 in Los Angeles, there were many who refused to accept it as a sport. Many people viewed at as a form of ballet, except the performers swam, ducked underwater, held their breath and wore nose clips. But while people appreciate the grace and precision of the contestants, they fail to realize just how physically challenging it is, though this could be because most of the hard work takes place underwater. Performers have been known to train for six hours a day to prepare for a major tournament.

Part of the problem the sport has is due to its history, which errs on the side of showbiz rather than competitive sport. Annette Kellerman, an Australian swimmer, used to entertain spectators at the turn of the last century by dancing in a glass tank. The Canadians picked it up and slowly the sport spread across swimming clubs, before becoming recognized in the USA. Its big boost came in the 1940s with films like *Million Dollar Mermaid* starring Esther Williams, based on Kellerman's life. These so-called 'aqua musicals' were very popular and featured Williams in various synchronized swimming routines. Buoyed by celluloid recognition the sport grew and was a demonstration sport at a number of swimming competitions, and eventually at the Olympic Games. Despite howls of derision, the sport was accepted in 1984, featuring duet and solo competitions. This has now changed, however, and the only remaining competitions are team competition and the duet, both of which the USA and Canada have dominated right from the outset.

WHAT TO **WATCH**

Each team consists of eight swimmers – with two reserves – or two for the duet, who spend their time in a pool performing routines and have to be perfectly in time with each other when they are in the pool. The competition consists of a five-minute free programme, or four for the duets, where performers can come up with their own routines, and a three-minute technical programme, where set moves have to be completed in a set order. For both routines, the teams select their own music.

10 judges watch every move the swimmers make in the pool as they twist and turn in time to the music, all while avoiding to touch the pool floor or side.

In the free routines, swimmers must show creativity and flair, using the whole pool. This is the most spectacular aspect of the sport, where contestants will do all they can to impress the judges, using new moves devised through hours of practice and preparation. Before entering the pool, swimmers can spend 10 seconds on the edge, called deckwork. This is not judged, and is merely used to give a good first impression.

WHAT ARE THE **RULES?**

Judges award points in both the free programme and the technical programme for technical merit and artistic impression.

There are 10 judges in all, five scoring technical merit and five scoring artistic impression. The maximum they can award is 10 points, and can award the scores in one-tenth of a point increments, for example, 6.3. Those judging technical merit look for how synchronized the swimmers are, their movement and position in the water, and the difficulty of what they are attempting to do.

Those judging artistic impression look for the creativity and flair in the routine and unlike judges scoring technical merit, they will judge on overall feel. They will also consider how well the music fits the performance.

Scoring is quite complex once the judges have made their decisions. First of all, the highest and lowest of the scores within each group of five judges are discarded, and the remaining three are averaged out. The technical merit score is multiplied by six, the artistic merit score is multiplied by four. The two totals are added together to give an overall score for the routine.

It does not end there. The free routine is more important so that score is multiplied by 0.65, while the technical routine is multiplied by 0.35. The two sums are added together to give the final score. Luckily, there is an electronic programme to add everything up.

In Sydney, eight teams will contest the team event and 24 teams will compete in the duet. The latter perform in a preliminary competition to narrow the field to 12.

WHO WILL **WIN?**

Great Britain will not be there. All four gold medals in the past have gone to the USA or Canada, and they will again be tough to beat. However, there are signs that the balance of power is shifting across to the eastern side of the globe. At last year's World Championships, Russia claimed the team gold, followed by Japan, with Canada and the USA relegated to third and fourth respectively. It is a similar story in the duets. The highest US placing was fifth, with Canada sixth, with the Russian pair Olga Brushnikina and Maria Kisseleva taking gold, and Miya Tachibana and Miho Takeda of Japan grabbing silver.

DID YOU **KNOW?**

- Although it may look as if they are, the swimmers do not wear swimming caps. Instead they use gelatin to keep their hair in place.

- As most of the routines are spent underwater, speakers are placed beneath the surface so the music can be heard at all times, though it is muffled.

- Above the water there is a limit to how loud the music can be played. 90 decibels is the general limit, sometimes rising to 100 decibels for the occasional crescendo.

- The swimmers do not have to be synchronized when they enter the water.

- It may be an all-female sport now, but the first recorded synchronized swimming event was actually performed by men in 1891. They were known as 'artistic swimmers'.

Table Tennis

16 – 25 September, State Sports Centre

For most of us, a table tennis bat is a simple implement, but for the best players in the world it is a highly-refined piece of equipment. The days when ping-pong (or even flim-flam as the game was once known) was played with cigar boxes and a carved champagne cork for a ball by English gentlemen after a protracted dinner are long gone. Now, the bats are made out of wood covered with a layer of sponge, topped with a piece of rubber chosen to suit a player's specific style and array of shots. A new piece of rubber is used in every match, giving players different controls of speed and spin. Indeed, some glues used on the 'paddles', as the bats are commonly known, are banned in international competitions because they can make the hollow, celluloid ball travel up to 30mph faster than usual.

People with limited experience of table tennis will be surprised at how fiercely competitive the professional game is. All sorts of psychological ploys are used to put off an opponent, though explicit unsporting behaviour is punished. Aggressive stances at the table, staring opponents out, towelling off or tying one's shoes to deliberately slow up play are all common practice. The game is now dominated by the Asian countries, in particular the Chinese, whose mastery of spin and astonishing agility around the table can make them virtually unbeatable. The Europeans controlled the sport in the early part of the last century, but since the sport entered the Olympics in 1988, nine of the 12 gold medals have gone to China.

It is also one of the fastest-moving sports in the Olympics. To stop matches turning into defensive wars of attrition – the organizers have no time for something as dull as defence – a unique 'expedite system' is used. After 15 minutes of play the umpire will stop a rally in mid-shot (unless 19 or more points have been scored) and start the expedite system, meaning that the serving player must win a point by the thirteenth shot of the rally or forfeit the serve to his opponent. The only exception is when both sides have scored at least 19 points, because this means that they have been playing quickly enough and so everyone is happy. Table tennis matches used to last hours, now if you blink, you can miss a game.

WHAT TO **WATCH**

The ball is 1½ inches in diameter and is played on to a 9-foot × 5-foot-wide table with a six-inch-high net stretched across the middle. The actual playing area is 40 feet in length, leaving 15½ feet for moving about at each end of the table – and players use every inch of it. One of the more thrilling parts of the game occurs when a player is forced to the back of the playing area yet still manages to land what is a tiny ball, with heavy spin applied, on to the opponent's side of the table. Footwork is critical, and agility a must, to return a ball travelling at 100mph. Attacking players will stay close to the table and force their opponent to the back of the court before attempting a drop shot or unstoppable smash, while a defending player will let the opponent do all the hard work and frustrate him into making an error by being difficult to beat.

In Sydney, there will be four table tennis events, men and women's singles and doubles. Matches are the best of five games. In the singles the seeded top 16 advance while 48 others contest a qualification round, of which 16 advance. The last 32 then play an elimination tournament. The same format is used for the doubles, but with 32 teams involved.

WHAT ARE THE **RULES?**

The first player to reach 21 points wins the game, though if the score is 20 points all, the game must be won by two clear points, so play continues until that happens. Each rally begins with a serve, which must be hit from behind the end line and from above the table. The ball must be tossed at least 16 centimetres up in the air using the non-paddle hand and hit on its descent. The ball must bounce on the server's side of the net before bouncing on the opponent's side. In singles, the serve can be directed anywhere on the table, though in doubles it must always go diagonally from right-hand corner to right-hand corner. The receiver returns it, then the servers' partner must strike it next followed by the receiver's partner. Play must continue in this sequence throughout the rally, and those who hit out of turn lose the point. After every five points, service is changed for both singles and doubles.

Other rules include:

- A return that touches the net then lands on an opponent's side of the table is declared good.

- The unplayable shot, one where the ball bounces right on the edge of the opponent's side of the table before flying off at an unexpected angle, is declared good.

- If a player touches the table with their free hand, or touches the net, they lose the point.

- If the ball strikes a player's body or item of clothing while the ball is over the table then they lose the point.

- Players must not hit the ball before it bounces on their side of the table.

- If a player bumps into the table with enough force to make it move, then they lose the point.

WHO WILL **WIN?**

Expect a Chinese whitewash in this event. The Chinese take this event more seriously than any other, including the World Championships, and prepare very thoroughly. The favourite for the men's singles is the defending champion Liu Guoliang, who will be challenged strongly by his compatriot Kong Linghui for the gold. The best European hope lies with Vladimir Samsanov of Belarus and 1992 gold medal-winner Jan Ove Waldner of Sweden. Britain has no realistic hope of a medal. The best chance lies with Matthew Syed, but his results against Asian opposition have been poor in the past and reaching the last 32 would be a significant achievement.

In the women's singles, bet on Wang Nan of China to pip Li Ju for the title, with the best European being Tamara Bros of Croatia, though the quarter-finals may be as far as she gets. Korea's Ryu Ji Hye is one to watch, and is rated as very good. In the men's doubles, reigning champions Kong Linghui and Liu Guoliang should win, with Werner Schlager and Karl Judrak of Austria carrying European hopes. Clear favourites for the women's doubles are Wang Nan and Li Ju, who should only be troubled by compatriots Yang Ying and Sun Jin.

DID YOU **KNOW?**

- Players are allowed to inspect their opponent's paddle prior to a match to check it complies with the rules.

- Players wear shoes more akin to ballet slippers than trainers, enabling them to dance round the table.

- Players must not wear white clothing because it would hamper their opponent's ability to follow the white ball.

- At the World Championships in 1932, two players took part in a single rally that lasted one hour.

JARGON BUSTER

Blade: The face of the paddle that makes contact with the ball.

Block: In response to the powerful looping, topspin game (see Loop, below), the best players have mastered a response in the form of a block executed with a closed paddle face, which is held almost parallel to the ground. Blocking tactics are aimed at deflecting the power of the attacker's shot and are conducted close to the table using short strokes to strike difficult angles and unexpected parts of the table.

Counterloop: A European innovation during the early 1990s, the counterloop allows Olympic-level innovation during the early 1990s, the counterloop allows Olympic-level players to battle for control of the table against strong loop attacks (see Loop, below). By retreating about four feet from the table, players have developed an athletic counterlooping stroke that resembles the motion of a discus thrower. These rallies are among the most exciting encounters in today's fast-paced game where players have less than two-tenths of a second to read and react to an attacking shot.

High-toss serve: Originally an Asian innovation, the high-toss serve is an extreme variation of the basic legal service. High tossers often throw the ball 15 to 20 feet in the air, using the speed of the falling ball to create more spin on the serve as it digs into the sticky rubber on the surface of the racket. High tosses also disrupt the timing of the receiver and allow the server to shield the contact point of the serve with the paddle until the last possible second as the ball falls close to his body.

Loop: Most Olympic competitors, especially men, base their attacking tactics on a heavy topspin attack (the loop) that is unique to table tennis as compared to other racket sports. Introduced in its modern form by Hungarian and Czech stars in the late 1970s.

No-spin serve: Given the heavy spin and great variation in the serves of elite players, the most deadly serve at Olympic level can, perversely, often be the serve that doesn't spin at all.

Speed glue: To enhance the effectiveness of modern rubber technology, world-class players prepare their rackets with a mixture of adhesive chemicals to attach their preferred rubber sheets to the sides of paddles. The glue remains damp throughout a match and enhances the power and spin players can generate upon a ball. This temporary turbo-charging effect only lasts for one match and must be replicated for each encounter. At full boost, a speed-glued racket can generate a speed of almost 100mph.

Taekwondo

27 – 30 September, State Sports Centre

Around 2000 years after the sport was first practised in Korea by the Koguryo dynasty, taekwondo takes its place in the 2000 Olympics. As one of the new Olympic sports, taekwondo will arouse great interest, though very few will know its troubled and chequered history. First evidence of the sport was found in mural paintings in royal tombs in Korea dating back to 37BC. It developed during Korea's long history, but as the national fortunes of the country deteriorated so did the sport. When Japan colonized the country in the early half of the twentieth century the practising of martial arts was strictly forbidden. But the practice carried on in secret and following the liberation of Korea after World War Two the sport was resurrected, and Korean instructors began travelling abroad to teach the sport. At Seoul in 1973 the first World Championships were held, with 19 countries participating. Now, the World Taekwondo Federation has 152 affiliated nations and the global taekwondo population is estimated at around 30 million people. After being adopted as a demonstration sport at the 1988 and 1992 Olympics, the ancient art of taekwondo is finally an Olympic sport.

Taekwondo experts state that the sport is defensive in spirit, since it was a martial art used as a defence against enemy attacks. It was also used to improve the physical condition of young men, aid their military training, and improve their self-confidence. One of the main tenets of the sport, as for other martial arts, is that its skills should never be used aggressively or in situations where the use of force can be avoided.

WHAT TO **WATCH**

In taekwondo, the whole body is used as a weapon, using hands, feet, elbows, knees or any other part of the body. It is well known for the spectacular combination kicks that can leave an opponent floundering, as well as a whole range of sharp, angular moves and flowing, almost balletic, movements. All bouts begin in a very friendly manner, with opponents bowing politely at each other, before battle commences. Once the referee shouts 'Shi-Jak!' to start the bout, however, the niceties end, as evidenced by the protective equipment contestants are forced to wear, including head, body and shin protectors, mouth and groin guards.

For the Sydney Olympics, the competition is split into four weight divisions for both men and women, as opposed to the eight traditionally used at the sport's World Championships. The divisions featured in Sydney are as follows: Men, under 58kg, under 68kg, under 80kg and over 80kg. Women, under 49kg, under 57kg, under 67kg, over 67kg.

WHAT ARE THE **RULES?**

A contest involves two 'fighters', one blue (Chung), the other red (Hong). They contest the bout on a 12-metre-square mat, within which is an eight-metre-square area where the main action takes place. A four-metre-square area (inside the eight-metre-square area) is known as the alert area and if both contestants step into it the bout is stopped. The aim is to try and score points by landing kicks on the opponent's head and body, or punches to the body. The bout lasts three rounds of three minutes each with a one-minute break between each round. A competitor can win by knocking their opponent out, by scoring the most points, by default, if the opponent earns three penalty points or if an opponent is disqualified.

One point is scored for each legitimate strike. A strike is considered legitimate if two or more of the three judges considers it meets the following two criteria:

- If it is delivered to a scoring area on the opponent. These are the head, the abdomen and each side of the body. All three are marked on the opponent's body protector. Strikes below the abdomen are forbidden and penalized.

- If it is delivered with the permitted parts of the body. Kicks to the head and body must be struck with parts of the foot below the ankle, while blows to the body must be done with the front of the index and middle finger knuckles of correctly clenched fists.

Penalties play a major part in any bout. There are two types, known as kyong-go and gam-jeom. The former, a warning, occurs most regularly and costs a contestant a half-point penalty, though it does not count unless the offender errs again and is warned, making a whole point. It is awarded for offences such as grabbing, holding, feigning injury, pushing, and turning the back on an opponent.

The gam-jeom is a more serious offence, and leads to one point being deducted. This penalty is awarded when a competitor throws another, deliberately steps over the boundary line, pulls an opponent to the ground by grappling with their foot in the air or fiercely attacks the opponent's face with the hands.

As in boxing, when an opponent is knocked to the ground the referee begins a 10-second count. In taekwondo, however, a knockout occurs if any part of a contestant's body touches the floor apart from the foot. The referee can also administer the count if a competitor is unwilling to continue. The referee counts in Korean until reaching eight, which is mandatory whether the competitor is ready to continue or not, before deciding whether the bout should go on. If he does not the other contestant wins by a knockout.

If a contest ends in a tie on points, then the person with the most points before penalties were deducted is declared the winner. If the bout is still tied, it is the referee who decides who has won the fight on the basis of which fighter has showed the most willing. The only exception occurs in the final, when a tied bout will go to an extra, sudden death round where whoever scores first wins. If no result is achieved the final decision once again lies with the referee.

Other main rules include:

- If both contestants are knocked down and fail to recover by the end of the count then the highest point scorer wins.

- A point can be taken away if a contestant commits an offence immediately after earning a point, such as falling deliberately to the floor to avoid a counter-attack.

In Sydney, all the bouts in each division will be straight knockout bouts until the final. The bronze medal is contested between all those defeated by the two finalists. The two losing semi-finalists go through automatically, while all the other losers fight it out in two pools, with the two pool winners going through to meet the two unsuccessful semi-finalists. The two winners from those bouts then meet to contest the bronze medal.

WHO WILL **WIN?**

Britain has a very real prospect for a medal in the shape of 16-year-old Sarah Stevenson, likely to be the youngest member of Britain's Olympic team. She is currently world junior champion and European senior champion. It would be a fantastic achievement if she were to win a medal in the first ever Olympic taekwondo competition. North and South Korea, as many would expect, are the ones to beat. They possess the contestants everyone will fear, with Iran and Turkey not far behind in the men's tournament. Taipei and China are going for gold in the women's. At the 1999 World Championships, South Korean flyweight Jong-Il Yoon and Chinese bantamweight Wang Su, took the men's and women's 'most valuable player' awards respectively.

DID YOU **KNOW?**

- Taekwondo is a number of ancient martial arts unified into one sport. It translates as 'the ways of hands and feet'.

- If a contestant is knocked out by a kick to the head they are forbidden from competing again for 30 days.

Tennis

Olympic tennis had great difficulty luring top players to enter the tournament since it was re-established at the Games in 1988. No prize money, no ranking points, and in the middle of the summer when much more cash can be made elsewhere, it was not surprising that the world's best turned their noses up at the tournament. Now, things have changed as the tournament has established itself and the idea of winning a gold medal appeals more than a sackful of cash. It appears Pete Sampras, Andre Agassi, Pat Rafter and Tim Henman will all be playing in Sydney, making tennis one of the Games' highlights.

The court at Sydney Olympic Park will suit the powerful players. It is a synthetic rubber hard court that promises to be very fast, ideal for big servers such as Great Britain's Greg Rusedski.

Modern tennis has a strange history. It was invented by Major Walter Wingfield in 1873 and introduced at English garden parties, where it was known as Sphairistike, from the Greek word for ball. Major Wingfield acknowledged that he had adapted an ancient version of handball, but he was the man who brought in changes, the most important being the net. Tennis took off in the USA and Australia and was included in the very first Games of 1896 and continued until 1924 until the familiar amateurism versus professionalism row reared its ugly head. It did not help that the Olympics often clashed with the greatest tennis tournament of all, Wimbledon, and the result was that it languished in the Olympic wilderness for 64 years until 1988 when professionals were actively encouraged to compete. Steffi Graf turned up and helped herself to a gold medal, but it was not until 1996 that most of the world's best decided to play, and Andre Agassi took the men's gold.

WHAT TO **WATCH**

Olympic tennis uses the format of all other professional tournaments. Players are seeded according to their world ranking and then a draw is made. All matches are elimination rounds until the semi-finals. The two semi-final winners play for gold and silver, the two losers compete for the bronze. The singles will have 64 entrants, the doubles 32. There is no mixed doubles tournament.

For the uninitiated, players serve from the baseline (the back line) from one side of the court to the other. The serve must land in a box diagonally opposite the server and avoid the net. If not, a fault is called unless the ball clips the net and still lands in the box, in which case a 'let' is called and the serve is retaken. If a player faults twice, a double fault, on one serve then they lose the point. Service games alternate throughout the match. The serve must be returned over the net and the rally continues until one player is unable to return the ball.

WHAT ARE THE **RULES?**

All men and women's matches, except the men's final, are played as the best of three sets, so the first to win two sets takes the match. The men's singles and doubles final are best of five sets. A set is won by winning six games, though it must be by two clear games. If not then a tie-breaker is played, where the first person to seven points is declared the winner of the set. The only time the tie-breaker is not played is in the final set of a match, known as an advantage set. On these occasions play continues until one side has won by two clear games, so there could be a repeat of the men's doubles semi-final in Atlanta 1996 when Australians Todd Woodbridge and Mark Woodforde won the final set 18-16 before going on to claim gold.

WHO WILL **WIN?**

British hopes lie with Greg Rusedski and Tim Henman in the men's singles. Rusedski has been dogged with injury recently and will be hoping he is at his physical peak since the fast surface in Sydney will suit his game, which is based around an immensely powerful serve. Henman is inconsistent, looking like a world-beater one minute and an amateur the next. At his best he is a match for anyone in the world though he can struggle against lesser players, so getting through the first couple of rounds will be very important. If he gets through to the last eight he could go on to win a medal.

The top 48 players in the world after Wimbledon 2000 will be invited, with a maximum of three players per country. This means Pete Sampras will be there and if he is fit and eager he could win the only major tennis title he has not won. However, Andre Agassi is back at his best and is also a good bet, as is the highly-talented Russian Yevgeny Kafelnikov, who can be unstoppable if on good form. The players everyone will be worried about, however, are the Australian pair, Pat Rafter and Mark Philippoussis. With fanatical home support and experience of what could be energy-sapping conditions allied to great personal ability they will be very hard to beat.

The women's tournament could be more entertaining than the men's – it often is. The long-running saga between the Williams sisters, Venus and Serena, and Martina Hingis looks set to continue in Sydney. Little love is lost between them so watch out for some fireworks. The only real threat to these three, unless someone springs a major surprise, is America's Lindsey Davenport, the 1999 Wimbledon champion and defending Olympic gold medallist.

DID YOU **KNOW?**

- Andre is not the first member of the Agassi family to compete in the Olympics. His father was part of the Iranian boxing team.

- Players can return the ball by hitting it around the net even if it is lower than net level as long as it lands within the boundaries of the court.

- The electronic eye, the highly unreliable beeping machine that is supposed to detect a service fault, is not being used in Sydney. Instead, the service lines will be replaced with electronic detectors to give a more reliable idea of whether a ball is 'in'.

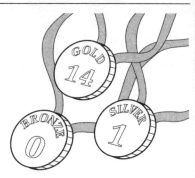

Triathlon

16 – 17 September, Sydney Opera House

Together with taekwondo, the triathlon is one of the new sports at the Sydney Games, though the history of both events could not be more dissimilar. While taekwondo is an ancient sport, refined over thousands of years, the triathlon is little more than a quarter of a century old. Put simply, it is a massive test of endurance for all those who dare to enter it, since it is comprised of a 1.5-kilometre swim, a 40-kilometre bike ride and then a 10-kilometre run in straight succession. Add to the mix what could be soaring Sydney temperatures and you get a gruelling test of stamina.

The sport has a colourful past, despite its young age. It was developed in 1973 as a way of providing track runners with new methods of extending their endurance. A year later, in San Diego, the first official triathlon event was held, but it was not until 1978 that it came to public attention, in an event known as the Hawaii Ironman. This was set up by three American marines to discover who was the best athlete; was it the one who competed in the Honolulu ocean swim, the one who competed in the Oahu round-the-island cycle race, or the runner who entered the Honolulu marathon? To find out, they decided to tackle all three sports in succession, and so one of the most punishing sports ever was born. The Ironman is still run today, featuring a 2.4-mile swim, a 112-mile bike ride and a run over marathon distance. They must all be mad.

Each of the disciplines requires an intense training schedule that can put immense strain on the athletes. This was highlighted recently when one of the sport's giants, and a favourite for gold in Sydney, the Australian Greg Welch, was forced to retire with a heart problem which he first noticed in competition. He will miss out on what promises to be one of the most picturesque events in the Games – the athletes swim, cycle and run around Sydney harbour and the Sydney Opera House foreshore.

WHAT TO **WATCH**

For the purposes of competition, including the Olympics, distances have now been standardized to aid comparison with past events.

The race begins with a mass start and then continues with no stopping whatsoever. After completing one leg of the race athletes merely run to the start of the next leg. As in a relay race, smooth changeovers are vital; a second dropped while attempting to get on a bike can cost a race. Men usually finish the whole race in around 1hr 50mins (20 minutes for the swim, 60 minutes for the cycle leg and 30 minutes for the run), while the women expect to complete the course in just over two hours. The women's race will take place on the first morning of the Olympics, with the men's following the day after, a perfect chance for the sport to showcase itself in front of the world.

Cycling - Chris Boardman (GBR)

Cycling - Lance
Armstrong (USA)

Modern Pentathlon - Kate Allenby (GBR)

Rowing - Steve Redgrave and Matthew Pinsent (GBR)

Swimming - Ian Thorpe (AUS)

Swimming - Susan O'Neill (AUS)

Tennis - Tim Henman (GBR)

Tennis - Greg Rusedski (GBR)

Tennis - Andre Agassi (USA)

Tennis - Martina Hingis (SUI)

Triathlon - Simon Lessing (GBR)

Wrestling - Alexander Karelin (RUS)

The first person to complete the whole course is declared the winner. The swimming leg starts both the men and women's event, with the competitors diving en masse into the water from a pontoon. The course is marked out using buoys and ropes. Cutting any corners incurs stiff penalties. Athletes can perform any swimming stroke they want, though nearly all choose to do the fastest stroke, the crawl.

Once they emerge from the water, the athletes get on their bikes. If an athlete gets a flat tyre they are permitted to run with the bike to a tyre-change station, but otherwise they must remain on the bike at all times. Riders are allowed to ride in the slipstream of the cyclist in front, a practice known as drafting, and will take turns to cycle at the front to keep up a steady pace.

Strange as it may sound, the most important rule for the running section is that athletes must complete the course on foot. This is because in some events, due to their gruelling nature, athletes have been known to cross the finishing line crawling on their knees. This is forbidden in the Olympics.

The rules are most strict when dealing with changeovers between disciplines. No one can impede another athlete during this time, or interfere with an opponent's equipment. Athletes must only use their own bicycle rack, and return their bike to it after finishing the cycling leg. They must fasten their helmet and not take it off until the bike is back on the rack. Athletes must only mount or dismount their bikes at a designated line, and cannot cycle their bikes in the change-over (transition) area.

Penalties are awarded if an athlete impedes another. If this occurs during the swimming leg then the offender is made to stop for 30 seconds at the end of the leg before continuing. During the cycling leg an official may warn a competitor with a yellow card, meaning the athlete must stop and await the official's permission to continue. Two yellow cards leads to a red – and disqualification.

50 athletes will contest both the men and women's event, with no nation allowed more than three competitors in each event.

WHO WILL **WIN?**

Great Britain has a fine history in the triathlon and has a great chance of winning medals, particularly in the men's event. Simon Lessing is placed highly in the International Triathlon Union's rankings and last year finished second in the World Championships, with another Briton, Andrew Johns, finishing fourth. Lessing is rated as a good all-rounder, but is particularly strong in the running leg. Both men will be looking to challenge a strong Australian threesome, which will include Greg Bennett and Chris McCormack, while world champion Dimitri Gaag of Kazakhstan and Hamish Carter of New Zealand will also be strong contenders.

Britain also has a chance in the women's event, although the Australians are extremely good. They took the first five places in the last World Championships and either Loretta Harrop, Emma Carney and Jackie Gallagher will probably win. Britain's Sian Brice was the highest-placed non-Australian at the Championships and will be hoping for a medal, while attention will also be on Michelle Dillon who won her first major competition at the end of last year. Steph Forrester may also be competing and hoping to gain valuable experience.

DID YOU **KNOW?**

- Nudity, or indecent exposure is forbidden. This may sound strange, but can be a problem when athletes are rushing to peel of wetsuits, put on helmets, take off shoes and pull bikes off a rack. Accidents often happen.

- Appropriately, the name of the man who set up the first competition for this punishing sport was called Dave Pain.

Volleyball

Beach Volleyball: 16 – 26 September, Bondi Beach
Indoor Volleyball: 16 September – 1 October, Sydney
Entertainment Centre

There used to be a popular sport named volleyball. It was not, as marketing people would say, a 'sexy' sport but it drew the crowds and provided fans with good entertainment and thrilling action. For years the rules stayed the same and nobody imagined much would change. But then people started playing the game on the beach, and the game quickly caught on. In our tabloid age, the concept of good-looking men and women playing sport in skimpy outfits on golden beaches was a winning idea, so the new game was called beach volleyball and a professional circuit was started. This, as the marketing men did say, was a sexy sport. Soon television companies and a host of sponsors were queuing up, and to everyone's surprise the sport was included in the 1996 Olympics where it proved very popular. Poor old traditional volleyball was ignored by everyone and slunk away from the Games unnoticed, but vowing to return, bigger and bolder, and take on its errant offspring.

This is really the history of volleyball over the past 10 years. But in order to regain its popularity, volleyball returns to the Olympics as a radically revamped game. The indoor game has created a new position, called the 'libero'. This is a specialist role aimed at introducing longer rallies into the game and more spectacular defensive play. The libero will wear a different colour from their team-mates, can come on the court at any time and their role is to get low to the ground, dig out shots from the opposition and set up counterattacks for their home team. The libero, however, cannot serve, spike (hit attacking shots at the net) or play in the front line. Their presence at the back of the court should mean volleyball rallies are more flowing and pulsating than before.

However, this is not the only rule change in the game. Instead of only being able to score when serving, the organizers have decreed that either side can score a point on every rally, regardless of who is serving, making a fast game even faster. It is a far cry from the day, just over 100 years ago in Massachusetts, USA, that William Morgan invented the game as a less strenuous alternative to basketball. It entered the Olympics in 1964 and has been a feature ever since. Indoor volleyball's fight back starts here.

Beach volleyball has a more curious history. It began as family fun on the beach, before, legend has it, becoming the chosen sport of a French nudist colony. The Americans picked it up and played it on Sorrento Beach in Los Angeles, drawing spectators like The Beatles and Marilyn Monroe, who gave it the glamour it needed to become a mainstream TV sport in the USA. In 1987, a World Championship was established, followed by a world series that attracted huge crowds. In 1993, the women's World Championships got underway, and in 1996, it was included in the Games. Its rapid rise has not stopped the organizers trying to grab even more of the limelight and television ratings, though. For

Sydney, where the tournament will be held on Bondi Beach, volleyball officials have decided to restrict the size of the competitors' swimsuits so that as much flesh as possible is on show. Not everyone is going along with this. The Australian side has registered their concerns, pointing out that the Olympics are being held in the Australian equivalent of spring, so it could be slightly colder than during the height of summer and they want to be able to wear tights. If they lose that fight, expect to see lots of goose pimples.

WHAT TO **WATCH**

Volleyball

There are six players in a volleyball team. The object of the sport is to make the ball hit the floor on the opponent's side of the net. Usually a player at the back of the court will bump the ball into the air for an offensive player at the net to 'spike' the ball into the opponent's court at speeds of up to 100mph. Players will often dummy the ball, leaving it for another in order to confuse the opposition's defence. Alternatively, rather than spiking, they may shape to smash the ball but instead delicately drop the ball just over the net, catching the other side out of position.

In defence a team will seek to block the spike, and with the new libero position, set up a counterattack. Players need to be agile, fast and be able to jump like basketball players. In fact, outside the basketball court some of the tallest Olympians will be competing in the volleyball.

Beach Volleyball

Beach volleyball players must be more versatile than their indoor counterparts. They must be able to serve, spike, bump, attack and defend because there are only two players on each side, and all this on the same size court as the indoor game. Some cynics argue that part of the sport's skill is being able to hurl yourself around the sand, returning lost causes, hitting unstoppable spikes, while all the time keeping your sunglasses on.

WHAT ARE THE **RULES?**

Volleyball

The players begin the match in a fixed position, the three front-row players close to the net and the three back-row players at the base line. A team may touch the ball three times in trying to get it over the other side of the net and on to the floor of the opposition's court to score a point. Players are not permitted to hold the ball, even briefly, and cannot hit it twice. Players can use any part of their body, not just the hands, to hit the ball. However, if the ball, for example, hits the thigh then the hand this is counted as consecutive hits and ruled a foul. Other fouls that lose a rally include touching the net during play or striking the ball out of play.

There is also a new scoring system for Sydney. The team who wins the rally wins the points. A match consists of five sets. In the first four sets, a team must win 25 points, by two clear points, to win the set. In the fifth and final set, the first team to reach 15 points, again by a two-point margin, wins.

Other rules include:

- Coaches are able to give instructions to a side during a match, though he or she must stand in a specified area.

- Liberos cannot spike, serve or play in the front-row.

- Six substitutions are allowed per set. Substitutes can enter the game only once per set, can only replace a player who started the match and then can only be replaced by that same player.

- Only front-row players may block a shot.

- A block does not count as a hit.

- Each team is allowed two timeouts per set.

In the 2000 Games, 12 men's teams and 12 women's teams will compete. Each will be divided into two pools of six and will play each other once. The top four teams from each pool go through to the quarter-finals where the competition becomes a straight knockout. The winners take gold, the losers silver while the other six teams play off for positions three to eight.

Beach Volleyball
Obviously, beach volleyball is played on sand. The basic rules are similar to indoor volleyball with a few exceptions:

- The players have no fixed positions.

- Teams can only score when they are serving. If they win a rally while defending, they win the right to serve.

- A block is counted as a hit.

- Players can attack from any position on their side of the court, and from any height.

- The teams swap sides every five points.

- No substitutions are allowed.

- The maximum time allowed between rallies is 12 seconds.

In the early rounds, winners are the first team to reach 15 points, in a one-set only game, though like the indoor game, a team must win by two clear points. For the medal rounds, it is the first team to win two sets. The first side to reach 12 points, again by two points, wins the first two sets. In the third set, however, a point is scored on each rally, regardless of who is serving.

The competition for both men and women will feature 24 pairs, who are seeded so that one plays 24, two plays 23 and so on. The 12 winners go through, while the losers play-off for the right to be one of the four best losers allowed through to the last 16, who then play a knockout tournament through to the end.

WHO WILL **WIN?**

Great Britain will have no representation in either the men's or women's indoor volleyball competition. However, most neutrals will be very happy if they see a repeat of the 1996 men's final between Italy and the Netherlands. The Dutch won a thriller by just two points in the final set after three hours of twists, turns and suspense. The Italians are still smarting from that defeat and desperately want a gold medal, a feat that has eluded them so far. Also strong are Cuba, Russia and the USA. In the women's event, Cuba are the team to beat, having won the last two gold medals. Their main rivals will be Brazil, Russia and China.

Britain does have a team in the beach volleyball women's event in the shape of Audrey Cooper and Amanda Glover, though there is no realistic chance of a medal. The pair will be hoping to improve upon the ninth position they achieved four years ago, a position they also attained in the 1999 World

Championships. The USA and Brazil dominate the sport in the women's division, with Australia the only team likely to upset their superiority. Brazil are just as strong in the men's division, with the USA, Argentina and Switzerland their main rivals.

DID YOU **KNOW?**

- A member of the USA's gold-winning pair in the men's beach volleyball event four years ago was Karch Kiraly, who won two indoor gold medals with the American side in the 1980s.

- In Atlanta in 1996, the beach volleyball event was the third fastest competition to sell-out.

- Indoor volleyball follows some very strict rules of etiquette. Individual players must shake hands and exchange small gifts, usually a sticker or pendant from their country, with the opposition before a game. Bad language is punished with a yellow card and a player coming on as substitute must hold up a paddle stating the number of the player being replaced and can only come on court when the referee gives approval.

- The women's final in 1972 in Munich was so close that the fourth set featured 24 consecutive service changes without either side scoring a point.

WATER

Polo

16 – 23 September, Ryde Aquatic Leisure Centre and
Sydney International Aquatic Centre

This is a particularly gruelling sport. During the four seven-
minute quarters players are not allowed to touch the side or
bottom of the pool. Water polo players can swim up to three
or four miles during a game while having to fend off the
attentions of the opposition, which can often take a very
physical form. While rough play is punished, most of the
players' bodies are submerged out of the view of the referees
so really anything goes. Holding, pulling players down under
water, grabbing, pushing, eye-gouging, and worst of all,
swimming trunk pulling, mean the game is not for the faint-
hearted. In fact, many top players wear two sets of swimsuits
to prevent them being put off their game when their trunks
are being pulled and wear ear caps to try to stop the opposition pulling their heads down underwater by their ears, and
to provide protection when their heads slap against the water
during a tackle.

An adequate description of water polo would be an aquatic
form of rugby, although it does also bear some resemblance
to football. What is certain is that water polo players need
the physique of rugby players, the agility of footballers and

the endurance of Olympic swimmers. And it is worth noting that the women's game, which is at last an Olympic sport, over 100 years after the men's game began, is no softer than the men's.

WHAT TO **WATCH**

The aim of the game is to pass the ball up the pool and shoot it into the opponents' net. Players go forward by carrying the ball in one hand while using the other to swim forwards, pass it to another member of their team or shoot it into the net. Dribbling is done by pushing the ball along the surface of the water by creating waves in the water with the head or chest.

The game revolves around the use of a player known as the 'hole man' or two-metre player. He stays two metres from the opponents' goal while the other five 'outfield' players spread out around him. They attempt to get the ball to him on almost every attack because he is the team's main scorer.

Quick and sharp passing is essential to get the ball forward quickly, while shots are hurled at goal at high speeds. They can be scored off any part of the body apart from a clenched fist. The ball gets more protection than is given to most of the players!

The sheer physicality of the game means fouls occur at regular intervals; in fact, fouls account for nearly all stoppages.

A game can last up to more than an hour, which means a lot of swimming and treading water.

WHAT ARE THE **RULES?**

At the outset, both teams line up on their goal line while the ball is placed in the middle of the pool on top of a buoy. The referee then blows the whistle, the buoy is retracted, and each team's fastest swimmers propel themselves up the pool to reach the ball first and gain possession. The game, like football, flows between defence and attack, with each side trying to manoeuvre a scoring opportunity. The defence can tackle the player holding the ball, which must be kept above the surface of the water. The attacking team has 35 seconds from gaining possession in which to shoot. If the time expires then the ball passes over to the opposition.

Ordinary fouls include failing to shoot in time, touching the ball with two hands, taking the ball underwater and tackling an opponent who does not have the ball. A penalty foul occurs when a man is fouled by a defender within a line four metres from goal and results in a penalty throw from that distance, which only the goalkeeper can attempt to stop. An exclusion foul, given for unsportsmanlike behaviour, results in a player going to the exclusion area for 20 seconds. This allows the opposition a chance to score a goal using their extra-man advantage. Most goals are scored in this way.

If the scores are level at the end of the game then two periods of three minutes extra-time are played. If no side has won then a sudden-death period is played, and the first team to score wins the tie.

The game is played in a 50-metre pool and the water must be at least two metres deep throughout. Floating buoys make up the lines of the pitch, but all decisions rest with the referee. Red buoys indicate the two-metre line from each goal, yellow buoys the four-metre line and a green mark, the seven-metre line. The goals are three metres wide and 90 centimetres high.

Among the other major rules are:

- Players cannot pass the two-metre line they are attacking unless they are behind the ball.

- Goalkeepers are the only players who can use both hands to touch the ball.

- A bleeding player is ordered out of the game and substituted immediately.

- Substitutes may join the game at any time.

In Sydney, in the men's event, the 12 teams who qualify will be split into two pools of six. A round robin is then played and the top four in each pool advance into the quarter-finals where a straight knockout competition is played. The six women's teams play a round-robin preliminary round, with the top four teams going forward to play for the medals.

WHO WILL **WIN?**

Europe dominates the water polo competitions, and has done so since the sport was first included in the Olympics. Great Britain won three gold medals in the first part of the last century but has since faded and is unlikely to figure at all in Sydney. Hungary, who won four gold medals between 1932 and 1956, are extremely strong once again and will be battling it out with either Spain, the defending champions, or Italy, the 1992 champions. Russia and Australia have been playing extremely well in recent times and could be good outside bets.

DID YOU **KNOW?**

- Water polo is the joint oldest team sport in the Olympics, together with football.

- In the nineteenth century, the sport was so violent that several American universities banned it.

- During the 1994 World Championships, a fight started in the pool between Italian and Hungarian players that got so heated that the Italian coach jumped in the pool to join in. Six players were suspended as a result.

- One year later, the Hungarians beat the Italians 11–10 and bizarrely celebrated by dropping to their knees at the side of the pool and waddling in a line like ducks in order to taunt their rivals. It did not go down well with the Italians.

- Tarzan star Johnny Weissmuller, who won an Olympic swimming gold medal, also played for the American water polo team in the same Games.

JARGON BUSTER

Ball under: A technical foul; a player may not hold the ball underwater while being held or tackled by an opponent

Donut: A goal that is scored by a hard shot aimed at, or close to, the goalkeeper's head.

Double post: An attacking strategy that uses two players, one positioned in front of each goal post. Also called a double hole.

Driver: An attacking tactic, usually using a small player capable of fast, hard drives towards the goal and quick changes of direction

Dry pass: A pass made where the ball is caught without touching the water.

Eggbeater: A kicking stroke used for stability and support while treading water, also allowing the player to propel himself from the water to throw the ball unhindered. Similar to an alternating breaststroke kick.

Greenie: A quick shot taken by a perimeter player, following a pass from the two-metre man, in an effort to catch the defender and goalkeeper off guard.

Inside water: A situation in which the attacking player has an advantageous position in front of the defender, with nothing but open water between himself and the goalkeeper.

Slough: A defensive strategy whereby a player leaves the attacker he is guarding to check the move of another offensive player who is attacking from a more dangerous position.

Two-metre man: A player positioned in front of the opposing goal responsible for absorbing fouls, passing to team-mates and scoring; probably the most physically demanding position in the water. A two-metre defender tries to control the area in front of his team's goal.

Wet shot: A shot that is attempted while the ball is touching the water, using a quick wrist action. Also called an off-the-water shot.

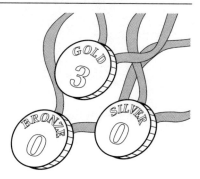

Weightlifting

16 – 26 September, Sydney Exhibition Centre

The weightlifting event has been changed for the Sydney Olympics. Not only have all the weight classifications been altered (meaning all the winning lifts will be new Olympic records), but more importantly, there is now a women's event. This will breathe new life into one of the oldest of modern Olympic competitions. It was included right from the start at the 1896 Athens' Games, though at that tournament there were no weight classifications. The person who lifted the heaviest weight, regardless of size, won the top prize and that was that.

Far more than any other sport in the Olympics, weightlifting is simply a display of pure, brute strength. It is a test of just how far a man or woman can push themselves while under immense pressure. Psychology plays a vital role – if a lifter does not believe he can lift a weight, it is certain he will not. Often in competition a lifter will come across a weight he or she has never lifted before, and it is the athlete who can overcome this challenge who will get the gold medal.

Weightlifting, like wrestling, dates back to ancient times. The sport evolved from simply lifting heavy weights, to the use of dumbbells, and now barbells, to hold the huge weights that are put on either side of the bar. In the mid-nineteenth century, weightlifting grew in popularity across Europe, leading to the first World Championship in 1891 and five years later it was included in the Olympics. However, it was not a permanent fixture until 1920, and it was only in 1932 that five weight classes and three types of lifts – the snatch, the clean and jerk and the press (see below) – were recognized. The latter was dropped in 1972, leaving just the snatch and the clean and jerk.

WHAT TO **WATCH**

The men compete in eight bodyweight divisions, newly established for these Olympics. The bodyweights given are the maximum allowed for each men's event – 56kg, 62kg, 69kg, 77kg, 85kg, 94kg, 105kg and over 105kg. The women compete in seven events – 48kg, 53kg, 58kg, 63kg, 69kg, 75kg and over 75kg.

There are two different types of lifts, the snatch, and the clean and jerk. Competitors must take part in both. In the snatch, the bar is lifted from the floor and over the lifter's head in one motion. The legs may be bent or split when lifting the bar but must come together for the lift to be declared valid by a panel of judges. In the clean and jerk, the lifter pulls the bar up to the shoulders in one movement, aided by dropping into a squat position, and then stands up straight. The next part of the lift involves jerking the bar to arm length above the head, splitting the legs in a forwards/backwards movement to aid the lift. Once the arms are locked and the bar is steady the lifters will bring their feet back together to ensure the lift is declared valid.

WHAT ARE THE **RULES?**

The rules are quite simple – the athlete to lift the heaviest weights in each division wins. Lifters are given three attempts to lift the weight in both the snatch and the clean and jerk. The heaviest successful lift in each category contributes towards the total score. So, if a competitor lifts 90kg in the snatch, and 130kg in the clean and jerk, their combined score is 220kg. If a lifter fails to complete a valid lift in their three attempts at the snatch, they can still compete in the clean and jerk but they will not receive an overall final placing.

If two lifters finish the competition with the same total then the one with the lower body weight is declared the winner. The weight of an athlete's proposed first lift determines their place in the starting order. If they choose to go for a light weight first then they will go early in the order. Many lifters attempt a weight they can manage safely before attempting a more challenging lift that will win them medals. Weights must increase by 2.5kg with each lift, unless an athlete decides to attempt a world record after securing gold. Once the lifters are on the platform they have one minute to complete the lift. Many use up most of that time, chalking their hands and psyching themselves up.

Three referees judge weightlifting. They signal a good lift by flashing a white light, and an illegal one by flashing a red one. A majority verdict is accepted as official, but a jury also watches each lift and may overrule the referees' decision.

There are a number of other rules to take into account:

- Lifting the bar in the squat position, to a position below the knees (the hang position) is not permitted. This prevents competitors from merely dangling the bar near the floor.

244

- If the bar stops at any time during the clean (the movement up to the shoulders) or the snatch or jerk (the movement above the lifter's head) then the lift is declared invalid.

- When the lift has been completed, a referee will tell a competitor to release the bar, but it cannot be dropped to the floor from above the waist.

- During the jerk, if a lifter shows any signs of trying to use the shoulders, lowering the body or bending the knees, before the lift is finished, a 'no lift' is called.

WHO WILL **WIN?**

Disappointingly, Great Britain failed to qualify any lifters for both the men and women's event due to poor results at last year's World Championships in Athens. For the women's competition China are the red-hot favourites, and many are predicting their lifters will sweep the board in Sydney. The only nations likely to prevent that happening are Taipei, Bulgaria, Nigeria and, with an outside chance, the USA.

The men's competition is likely to be more open, with Greece expected to do very well after their success in the World Championships. Bulgaria, Russia, the Ukraine, Turkey, Poland and China are also very strong. Individually, Greece's Pyros Dimas and Akakios Kakhiasvilis are both seeking to win their third consecutive Olympic gold medals.

DID YOU **KNOW?**

- In men's competition, the steel bar itself weighs 20 kilogrammes. Each weight placed on it is differentiated by using a colour scheme. Red is 25kg, blue 20kg, yellow

15kg, green 10kg, white 5kg, black 2.5kg and chrome 1.25kg. They are secured on to the bar by collars, weighing 2.5 kilogrammes each.

- The first recorded weightlifting event in Vienna in 1877 featured bizarre events such as lifting with hair and teeth, as well as the more conventional snatch and clean and jerk.

- One of the greatest weightlifters of all time, Turkey's Naim Suleymanoglu, who won three consecutive gold medals, could lift almost three times his own body weight. He weighed less than 64 kilogrammes.

BRITISH MEDAL COUNT

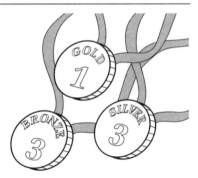

Wrestling

Greco-Roman: 24 – 27 September, Sydney Exhibition Centre
Freestyle: 28 September – 1 October, Sydney
Exhibition Centre

Wrestling is probably the oldest sport known to man, possibly as old as the human race itself. It was part of the ancient Olympics, where men with oiled bodies grappled with each other on sand. The founders of the modern Olympics wasted no time in incorporating this event, based on how they believed it was contested in 708 BC, into the modern Games when they were established in 1896. This version of the sport was called Greco-Roman wrestling, which the organizers believed was an exact replica of how the Greeks and Romans competed. Eight years later, 'freestyle' wrestling was added to the schedule, a more modern form of the sport but one that has proved even more popular than the original. This derived from a type of wrestling performed at fairs in England and the United States in the nineteenth century, known then as 'catch as catch can'. As its name suggests, it is a much more open, expressive form of wrestling.

Ancient wrestling has spawned many imitators, from the ancient art of 'sumo' wrestling in Japan, to the showbiz version practised by the likes of Hulk Hogan in America for the benefit of TV viewers. Olympic wrestling, needless to say, is the sport in its purest form and is contested by some of the fiercest and strongest men (and perhaps at the next Olympics, women) in the world.

WHAT TO **WATCH**

The main difference is between Greco-Roman and freestyle wrestling. In the Greco-Roman version, competitors can use only their arms and upper bodies to attack their opponent. Holding an opponent below the waist is forbidden. Freestyle wrestlers are allowed to use their legs to push, trip and lift opponents and can grab their rivals below the waist. As a result, Greco-Roman is a slower sport, involving two hulking opponents trying to use their massive upper body strength to hurl each other across the ring.

Freestyle wrestling requires more cunning and all-round strength and agility as the combatants have to circle each other before quickly moving in to deliver the winning hold or fall, while constantly avoiding attacks from the opponent.

WHAT ARE THE **RULES?**

The two versions are different in style, though there is little difference in the way they are judged and scored. The action takes place on an octagonal mat, which is specially marked. There is a circle seven metres in diameter, coloured yellow, which is the central wrestling area, followed by a one-metre-wide red circle known as the passivity area. This warns the wrestlers they are near the edge of the competition area. In the centre of the mat is a one-metre-wide area where the wrestlers start the match and return to when the referee commands it.

Given the close proximity of the two contestants, there are certain rules to prevent wrestlers gaining an unfair physical advantage. One is that fingernails must be short, to prevent scratching. A fully-grown beard is allowed, but stubble is not and players are required to shave on the day of competition if their whiskers are not long enough. Hair must be short or tied back, and arriving at the start covered in sweat or some other greasy substance is banned to stop wrestlers making sure they slip out of their opponent's grasp.

The objective in both sports is to bring down an opponent so he cannot move and his shoulders are pinned to the mat. This is known as a 'fall'. The match automatically ends if this is achieved. A victory can also be gained by winning 10 points in a bout (known as technical superiority) or by finishing the bout with more points (known as technical points). Each bout consists of two three-minute rounds, and to win at the end a wrestler must have scored at least three technical points. If that has not been achieved, or the points score is tied, then the bout goes into sudden-death overtime, where the next person to score wins. If no point is scored in three minutes then the judges pick their victor.

The most common ways of scoring points include:

- Takedown – This scores one point and occurs when a wrestler forces his opponent to the mat and takes control.

- Two points are awarded for turning an opponent's shoulders so that his back is facing the mat and his back is less than a right angle to the mat. This is known as the danger position. An extra point can be scored if the wrestler keeps his opponent in that position for five seconds.

- Three points are awarded for getting the opponent off his feet and swiftly moving him into the danger position, all in one movement.

- Five points can be awarded for risky moves, such as throwing an opponent through the air, which is always a crowd-pleaser.

There are a number of other rules that distinguish the two different forms of wrestling. These are:

- In Greco-Roman wrestling, a wrestler must fall to the mat with his opponent if he has forced his opponent down.

- In freestyle wrestling, locking the feet around the head, neck or body is not allowed.

Also:

- Wrestlers are not allowed to pull hair, ears or genitals, bite, kick, head-butt, strangle an opponent, touch his face between eyebrow and mouth, or use elbows or knees.

- Wrestlers cannot speak to each other during the bout.

- A wrestler is guilty of 'passivity' if he fails to initiate effective holds, or obstructs his opponent and prevents him wrestling. First a warning is given, and if it is not heeded then a point is given to his opponent.

- A wrestler guilty of foul play, cheating or anything deemed to be too brutal is disqualified immediately.

In Sydney, in both events, wrestlers compete in eight weight divisions, which are – 54kg, 58kg, 63kg, 69kg, 76kg, 85kg, 97kg and 130kg. Each division will contain 20 wrestlers, divided at random into six pools. Each wrestler will face the other in his pool, with the winners of the two four-man pools going through to the semi-finals, while the winners of the four three-man pools go into the quarter-finals. The two winners of the quarter-finals go through to the semi-finals to meet the four-man pool winners and the eventual finalists compete for gold and silver, while the two losers wrestle for the bronze.

WHO WILL **WIN?**

Great Britain's medals have all come in freestyle wrestling, with a vast majority of those earned at the contentious 1908 Games in London, where accusations of British bias were more common than the torrential rain that accompanied the event. This time it is hard to see us doing well in a sport that is dominated by the USA, Russia, Turkey and Iran.

The Russians, and nations that used to be part of the Soviet Union, dominate Greco-Roman wrestling. The biggest name in the sport is Russia's super-heavyweight Alexander Karelin, who will be seeking his fourth consecutive gold in Sydney. He is immensely strong and has devised a lift few of his opponents can resist. He picks them up and throws them over his head which, considering the size of the men he competes against, is astonishing. He is so good that most wrestlers believe scoring a point against him is a massive achievement.

DID YOU **KNOW?**

- All wrestlers must carry handkerchiefs during bouts. It dates back to the time when they were needed to wipe away blood, saliva and mucus during bouts, though now this is simply a tradition.

- In 1912, during the Greco-Roman event, a bout between Estonia's Martin Klein and Finland's Alfred Asikainen lasted for 11 hours and 40 minutes. The bout took place outdoors under a hot sun. Klein eventually pinned his opponent down but it was all too much. He was so tired he could not compete in the final and so got silver, with Sweden's Claes Johanson winning the gold by default.

- A doctor is on duty at every match and possesses the power to stop a bout whenever he believes a competitor is in danger.

BRITISH MEDAL COUNT

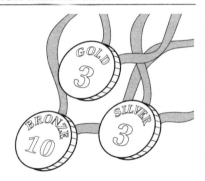

FOOTBALL CONFIDENTIAL
Ian Bent, Richard McIlroy, Kevin Mousley and Peter Walsh

Radio 5 Live's sports documentary team, *On the Line*, has spent the past five years unearthing football's most shocking secrets. *Football Confidential* contains the most startling of these investigations, from the grass roots of the park to the pinnacle of international football.

ISBN 0 563 55149 6
Price £6.99

...AND WELCOME TO THE HIGHLIGHTS – 61 YEARS OF BBC TV CRICKET
Chris Broad with Daniel Waddell
Foreword by Peter West

BBC Television has captured every great cricketing moment for more than six decades. *...and welcome to the highlights* looks back at these moments of sporting glory and how the BBC captured them for posterity.

Beginning with the very first broadcast by Teddy Wakelam in 1938 and ending with the 1999 World Cup Final, the book also contains unique interviews with many of the game's finest commentators and players.

ISBN 0 563 55123 2
Price £17.99

THE UNION GAME – A RUGBY HISTORY
Sean Smith

The Union Game – A Rugby History is the first book to explore the controversial history and development of rugby union from the game's origins to the advent of professionalism.

Exclusive photographs and interviews with the Union's all-time greats make *The Union Game* an essential guide to this exhilarating sport.

ISBN 0 563 55118 6
Price £16.99

BORN TO BE RILED
Jeremy Clarkson

Born to be Riled is a motoring milestone, the best of Jeremy Clarkson's writing in *Top Gear* magazine and the *Sunday Times*, now available in paperback. Only the most outrageous diatribes, the sharpest observations and the funniest experiences are included here in this souped-up, turbocharged collection of columns from Britain's most famous motoring journalist.

ISBN 0 563 55146 1
Price £6.99